The Talking Elephant

The Marvelous World of Elephants

Iythichanda Ramesh Uthappa

Translated from Kannada by: **PREMALATHA K.R**

AKSHARA MANTAPA
No. 1667, 6th Cross, 6th `C' Main Road
Hampinagar, Bengaluru - 560104

THE TALKING ELEPHANT
-The Marvelous World of Elephants

Written By :
Iythichanda Ramesh Uthappa
Mysore
Mob: 94830 49005

Translated By:
Premalatha. K.R

Published by:
Chetan Kanabur
Akshara Mantapa
1667, 6th Cross, 6th `C' Main,
Hampinagara,
Bengaluru-560104
Mob: 99861 67684

First Impression: 2021
Pages: 128
Book Size : 1/8 Demi
Price : Rs. 200

ISBN : 978 - 81 - 954061 - 5 - 9

Paper Used : 70 GSM Maplitho
Copies: 1000

Cover Photo : **K P Sathyanarayan**
Police Inspector, Karnataka State

Design : **Arun Kumar. G**

DEDICATION

Ajay Desai

The Elephant Man

MARVELOUS

The marvelous world of elephants is really a marvelous book. It exceeded my expectations. When ever we talk of elephants, it will be always about Dasara elephants, so when the author Itichanda Ramesh Uttappa, who is also a journalist asked me to write a foreword. I thought the book would be only about Dasara elephants. It is highly commendable that the author has written such a wonderful book about elephants other than Dasara elephants.

This is not fiction, but is the story of elephants that lived amongst us. When people achieve, we create webseries and cinemas, we write books about them and document their stories. But rarely elephants achievements and their life history is documented. In this context this is a marvelous book about the world of elephants. In this book, the achievements of each elephant, their pain, their love and their sensitivity touches the heart and it is hard to believe elephants can be like this. I believe once the reader starts reading this book, he will not keep it aside until the last page is finished. He has documented the achievements and feelings of the elephants that have been gifted and sent overseas. All the stories in the book are admirable and author has given interesting magical touch to all the events he has narrated. I am not simply praising, but I am suure the reads will agree with me after reading this book. I have known Ramesh Uttappa since the time I served as conservator of forests in Kodagu. Especially thses elephants have brought us close to each other. Sometimes Elephant human conflict reaches out of control in Kodagu. The role of media is important when the conflict is at its high. Ramesh uttappa's reports about this were excellent and were published based on facts with scientific analysis. Because of this he become one of my favorite journalists.

I was transferred to Bangalore as the director of elephant planning, he sometimes called me over phone to get information about elephants. From the beginning I have observed his innate curiosity about elephants. I came to Chamarajanagar as chief conservator of forests, Ramesh Uttappa contacted me and asked me to write foreward to his book about elephants. I was curious about elephants and while reading I felt I was wandering in the world of elephants, and was so engrossed in it, that I forgot to write the foreword. All the elephants in the book are well remembered for many days. This work is based on real events with rising Elephant human conflict everywhere this book is helpful in improving the relationship between elephants and humans. He has presented before us many interesting events which proves that elephants and Humans can live amicably even now. There is increased tendency to spoil relationships everywhere. Through these beautiful illustrations he has showed that humanity is beyond scientific analysis.

'Ambika', the elephant is the link to represent the relationship between India and America. Kaavan from Pakistan is the hero who the driving force behind the public movement led by animal lovers. The elder elephant 'lin Waang' introduces us to a war hero. It showed the Taiwanese how an elephant can inspire generations. 'Murthy' the lone tusker who was a Villain first, could be changed to become good by showing love. The story of the Imam who wrote his property to his elephants is mind boggling. In addition to these, the death of a pregnant elephant is disheartening. The author Ramesh Uttappa has documented such real stories which touches the heart. Everything here is unique and special. I believe these elephants are etched in the minds of the readers for ever.

This book will be close to the hearts of scientists, wildlife experts and animal lovers. Ithichanda Ramesh Uttappa has already written 25 different books. I wish this book also remains eternally in the minds of readers.

MANOJ KUMAR
Chief Conservator Of Forests
Chamarajanagara

ELEPHANTS ARE LIKE FAMILY MEMBERS

I was born in Kodagu (Karnataka state). Growing in the hilly regions. I was fascinated by elephants since childhood. When I was young, domestic elephants were hired from the neighbouring Kerala state to transport huge logsof wood. I was terrified of elephants and ran with fear when I came across one, without knowing if it was domestic or wild type. I could gather courage to see them only when elders assured me that unlike wild elephants domestic elephants had bells tied to their neck and were harmless. Trees were cut in the hill near my house and lumber was transported. It was not possible for lorries to access the road and reach the hill, so domestic elephants were employed to transport these huge logs down the road. I witnessed this scene with awe and was surprised to see a skinny man sitting on the huge elephant and controlling it. He looked like superman. I could not figure out how elephants understand our language and obeyed the Mahout, I even wondered why they remained subordinate to humans inspite of being strong. It was mystery to me!

I often visited Maletirike hill in our village and shuddered seeing wild elephants passing close by. I ran with fear when I saw elephant faeces, while loitering in the dense forests of the hill with my schoolmates. The elephants trumpet scared me.

When I was young, it was big news when wild elephants entered farm lands. In the beginning it was scary, but many years later, it was common to see elephants frequently visiting villages and were seen passing in front of houses. Why it entered villages is a moot question? Might be this was due to increase in the number of elephants or because elephants liked the taste of plantations. These elephants stayed put in the village for sometime and returned after few days. By then before leaving they would have farted upon banana, coconut and areca plants to their hearts content. Villagers were afraid to enter their farms because of elephants, it was scary to hear even a small sound. Our neighbouring village Palangala is located in the foot hills of the Maletiriki hill. Elephants are a common sight these days. They had even crushed few people to death and rendered a few handicapped. Many villagers in Kodagu are troubled by elephants, and here elephant human Conflict continues even to this day.

I am curious about this gigantic creature since I was a small boy. I was amazed to see them entering the villages. These huge animals come to villages from forests, crushed everything in front of our own eyes, destroyd harvest crops, ate them and returned back. The elephant repeated this by visiting the villages once in 3 months eating and returning. Later when I joined journalism, I could see domestic elephants from near. I have been to Dubare Camp and Mathigodu camp in Kodagu many times and have observed elephants closely. I love to learn about their behavior, their nature and to know their names, later when I became a journalist in Mysore,. I gained more knowledge of Dasara elephants. I visited the Mysore Palace daily for 2 months and become familiar with the palace elephants. Dasara elephants like Drona, Balarama, Arjuna, Kaveri, Sarala, Abhimanyu, Gopi, Dananjaya, Iswara, Gopalaswamy, Varalakshmi were dear to me like my own family members. During Dasara, all the reports from the Palace were only about elephants.

Later when I was assigned to study the life of PoomaleKudiya tribal Community who lived in the hilly regions, I got the opportunity to see wild elephants in their natural habitat I was surprised to know about the traditional knowledge of the tribes about elephants.

Especially these Kudiyas could easily trace the elephant in forests from far by their smell and they could accurately spot where the elephant was present. This is unique to them. I have tried many times, but could not sense the smell of elephants. By observing the direction of the wind they sensed the smell of elephants and gauged the exact distance from far, they could do this by experience. To safeguard themselves while moving in the forests they developed this sharp sense of smell. It is very difficult to encounter an elephant face to face and it is dangerous to confront elephants, but the tribal people feel totally unnerved, they are tactful and have their own way in dealing with such situations. It is impossible to avoid elephants directly, so the tribals run towards the back of the elephant, if it turns to attack them. They catch hold of the tail of the elephant in order to avoid its trunk and legs from hurting them. If it turns back to attack they turn around, with the elephant holding 'it's tail in their hand. The Elephant gets exhausted and becomes tensed, after many twists and turns and finally it gives up and escapes. This is a brave act indeed! But some people who are not brave enough. Panick at the sight of elephants. Few people react in a different way when they encounter elephants. They remove their clothes and throw it towards the elephants. In a fit of rage. The elephants start attacking and crushing the clothes. They run and escape diverting the attention of the elephant. This can be done by experience.

Once I was going to Mukkadlu, there I saw herd of elephants crossing Hattihole lake near Madapura. I was excited to see a tusker lifting a little elephant with it tusk while crossing. Like this I am always curious about elephants. Many years ago, I has written about the achievements and adventures of the elephant Abhimanyu. It had gone viral on social media. I have written many articles in Vijaya Karnataka daily about elephants present in various camps and also about Dasara elephants. I have also collected many facts about elephants. In 2020, the department of forests had conducted an online programme in collaboration with elephant project and I had Participated in the same. I have won first prize in quiz competition about elephants. Many people helped me by providing information regarding elephants. With all these experiences at hand. I ventured to write a book about elephants. Amazing facts about elephants, their special qualities, their achievements, about elephants that have earned fame abroad are all documented in this book. I have collected interesting stories about elephants. We always write about the achievements of humans, but forget to write about the 'elephants heros'. In this Context, I have written a different kind of book, where I have selected events that holds your curiosity from starting till the end. I have visited many places and collected much information about all the facts. I showed the manuscript of the book to Manoj Kumar. Chamarajanagar District chief Conservator of forests and asked for his advice. He gave proper guidance and had wrote a Preface to my book. I thank him for the same. My thank to friends Nagesh Panathale and Vignesh Bhootanadu who provided photos and to all those who are directly and indirectly helpful me in this venture.

I thank Sachin Krishna of Brahmi Creations's for Composing, I thank Senior Journalist Krishna Kumar and Shrinivas for their support in proof reading. I thank Chethan of Akshara Mantapa Prakashana, who published my book with love. This is my 26th Book. I believe you continue to encourage me like you did before your opinions are welcome.

Thanking You,

With Love

Iythichanda Ramesh Uthappa

Mysore

Mob: 9483049005

ROOTS OF ELEPHANTS BEHAVIOUR

This is a wonderful book by Iythichanda Ramesh Uthappa that says a lot about elephants. It is an interesting book that conveys a very profound message that elephants can be understood and they can blend with humans. In every Chapter of this book, he has mentioned about the life of elephants. It deals with facts and its purpose is to convey a great truth that elephants can be loved too. It also communicates some very fine material which every reader in every walk of life should understand. If we learn and apply the simple techniques revealed here in dealing with elephants, we will have proper knowledge about animals and elephants in particular. The author Iythichanda Ramesh

Uthappa's love for elephants was the direct inspiration for this book. His sincere efforts in collecting and explaining details about each elephant is amazing.

I have translated many books from Kannada to English. I am happy to have had the privilege of translating this book. Chetan who has cutting edge expertise in the world of publishing requested me to translate 'Aane Lokada Vismaya'.

This book takes the readers to the roots of elephants behaviour and explains various reasons for elephant human conflicts. While translating this book I made very few changes and did not alter any of the original content.

Enjoy reading this book and know more about elephants. As the author has rightly said, this is a unique book written about the achievements of elephants. It is not only Ramesh Uthappa's pleasure to write about elephants, but it is also mine to make this book reach to many animal lovers.

I thank Ramesh Uthappa and wish him all the best in his future Ventures.

Premalatha K R

THE KODAGU BEAUTY AMBIKA

EUTHANIZATION IN AMERICA

27TH MARCH 2020

Everyone stood there with a heavy heart. It was a touching moment, 'Ambika' once a beautiful elephant from Kodagu sent to America as a gift 59 years ago was going to be euthanized. No one wished this, but it was inevitable. The cynosure of all eyes and very much loved by the people of America was going to be laid to rest.

The doctors who had treated her for many years too came with a heavy heart. They were assigned to tranquilize first and then finally euthanize her. When the nodal officer signaled them, it was done. She slowly closed her eyes,

groaned slightly, stretched her arms and legs, her heart beat slowed and she laid still. People cried inconsolably, they tried to hug her, but the officers did not allow them because of covid 19 pandemic. What a helpless situation! They did farewell from far. The doctors walked out with their heads bowed down. Ambika, the Kodagu beauty was no more!

Ambika grew up in Kodagu. While young she was a sweet little toddler and was liked by all. In 1948, when she was eight year old, she was captured from Kodagu and taken by the department of forests. She soon became everyone's little darling. Always lively, she neither showed anger nor took up fight with people around her. She jumped with joy when she saw kids, and enjoyed playing with them all day. In a few years she become the honourable member of the forest department.

In 1961, when John F. Kennedy was the President of America, bilateral relationship between India and America was flourishing. To mark the sweet remembrance of this relationship, the Indian government took a decision to gift Ambika to Americans on behalf of all the kids in India. She was sent to America. Kids who played with her and people who enjoyed her company said goodbye with a heavy heart. There she found her abode and lived happily. Ambika became a proud Indian ambassador sent as a token of bilateral friendship.

She became a loving member of the Smithsonians National Zoo in Washington. Soon she adjusted to the new environment there. Her good behavior and manners attracted people and she became a friend to many. People visited the Zoo many times to meet and spend time with their loving friend Ambika.

She had spent 59 years in America, now she was old. In spite of her age related ailments, she was lively and upbeat. She had the reputation of being the one and the only elephant to be studied and experimented, in the whole world. She was the senior most member of South Asia's elephant clan which is oflate on the verge of extinction. Many labs have collected and preserved her blood samples and is being used to study in detail, the sound that elephants make, the changing sound of elephants in different situations, the speed of the sound, its fluctuations.

All these studies have been recorded and documented. One of the highlights of these studies was to know the main reason for the death of South-Asian elephants, and the difficulties they faced. Ambika has set the record as being the first elephant in the World to get GNRH hormone Vaccine administered to prevent fibroids in the uterus.

Ambika who gained much importance in her life, suffered age related health problems and she was well taken care of gradually her condition deteriorated, she could not stand with ease. It was a sore sight to see loving Ambika suffer. So the administrative board decided to euthanize her.

On march 27th 8.15 a.m, the euthanize process began and was complete by 9.15 a.m. Her mahout Mary Gayaalove who took care of her for 33 years wept inconsolably. "I was so sad when my mother died at a ripe age of 88 years, I am undergoing the same pain now after losing Ambika. Though this is a painfell and an unbearable loss, this was inevitable, because Ambika was tired. Now she is in peace" he cried.

Shanthi and Bhoji were the two elephants who were companies Ambika had in the same Zoo. When they were allowed to see Ambika after she was euthanized, they went round her for 15 minutes and tried to wake her up. When they realized she was no more, they wept silently and left the scene.

"May Ambika rest in peace. She came as a loving gift from India. 72 years old. She was the senior most of South Asian elephants, and she is no more" tweeted Sir Taaranjit Singh Sandhu the Indian Ambassador to America.

The Washington Post hightlighted the news of Ambika's death. Henceforth she is nothing but a remembrance.

THE RELEASE OF KAAVAN FROM PAKISTAN

This is a story that touches the heart, it was a successful fight against cruelty. The elephant was released from captivity of cruel people after a long fight for justice. This paved the way for healthy relations between man and wild life. This incidence showed the entire world that humanity, the all pervading spirit inspires our daily life. This successful fight for justice has no boundaries of countries, languages or religions.

The elephant's name is 'Kaavan'. Some call it 'Kavan', His was a tragic life. Loneliness is a great punishment faced by humans or animals. For no fault, Kaavan suffered for 41 years in solitary confinement, with no loved

ones. His life was unbearable because he was tied with chains for many years. He was finally released and sent to a different place and allowed to live with his companions. These are the events that occurred in Kaavan's life journey.

Kaavan, the elephant was put in one of the worst Zoos named Islamabad Zoo in Pakistan. In 1985, the Srilanka government gifted one year old sweet little elephant Kaavan as a token of love to the then Pakistan President Zia-ul-Haq. Pakistan government kept it in Islamabad Zoo. This was the beginning of his tragic life. It was all alone for 5 years in the Zoo after separation from its mother at an early age. Then in 1990, 'Sheli' a female elephant companion arrived from Bangladesh. Kaavan was very happy to play with her. But this happiness did not last long. Due to bad management in the Zoo, Sheli fell ill and died in 2012. Once again Kaavan was all alone. Added to this, the mahout who was supposed to take care of Kaavan with love and affection became a villain. Though a mahout, he had opened a petty shop outside the Zoo and would spend most of his time in the shop. In 2002 he complained the authorities that Kaavan had scared one of the

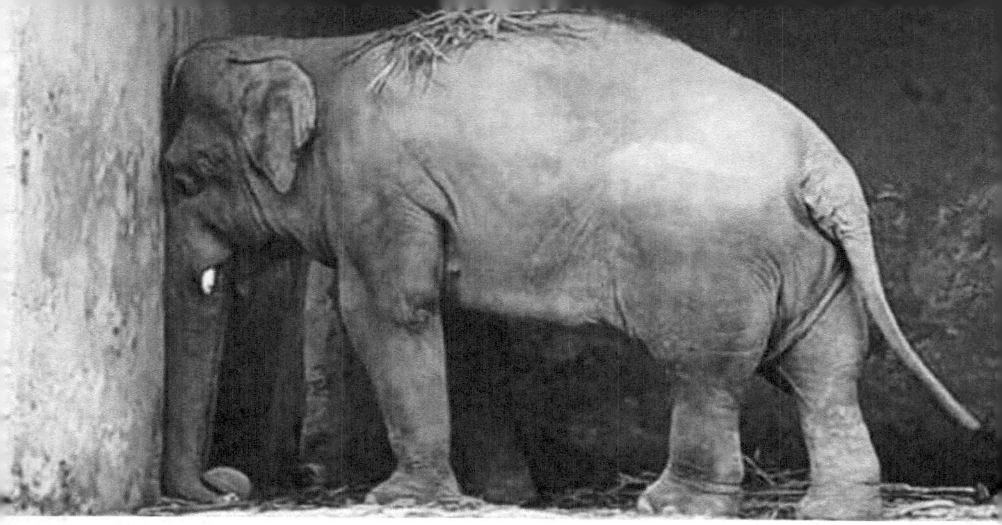

Zoo staff and so ordered to tie the legs of Kaavan with chains, for nearly 18 years. Kaavan lived in distress.

Kaavan was made to stand in the same place without any movement. No one took pity on this lonely elephant. He was depressed because he had lost his companion, Sheli and was all alone in captivity. Because his 4 legs were chained, he just moved his head and legs from where he stood. People who visited the Zoo thought he was dancing and they rejoiced and happily clapped their hands. But Kaavan was mentally affected and it was late when people understood about his loneliness and psychological trauma.

In 2016, this became worldwide news. Humanitarian reposts about the tragic life of Kaavan was published in newspaper. This became viral in social media. The repost about its loneliness and captivity for two decades made people angry. Worldwide enviromentalists, wildlife lovers were moved when they learnt of this. They started a movement "give justice to Kaavan". Nearly 2 lakh people participated and it became a historical movement.

Now, the government of Pakistan was alert. Till then they completely forgot about Kaavan's presence. Eventhen, the Islamabad administration didn't seem humane. Hundreds of e-mails poured in and people expressed their concern. Still

Kaavan was not completely released, only his 2 legs were removed from chains. Famous pop singer Cher took active part in this movement. She highlighted the issues in social media. And many people expressed solidarity beyond expectation and joined hands. The cry “Save Kaavan” was heard everywhere. Worldwide animal lovers protested in front of the Pakistan embassy. A petition was filed in Pakistan High Court requesting independence for Kaavan. After a long trial, the court gave a historical judgement. On March 21st 2020 Kaavan was granted freedom from captivity. According to the Court orders, the Srilanka government which gifted Kaavan was consulted and was asked to prepare a repost and decide where Kaavan can be sheltered. The Court then flayed the Zoo administration for the cruelty. Animal lovers worldwide rejoiced. They welcomed the judgement and animal lovers organisations joined hands with pop singer Cher and supported the movement. A few of them personally visited the Zoo and examined Kaavan's condition. Cher went to Pakistan, met the then Prime minister Imran Khan, the Zoo administrators and all the animal lovers there.

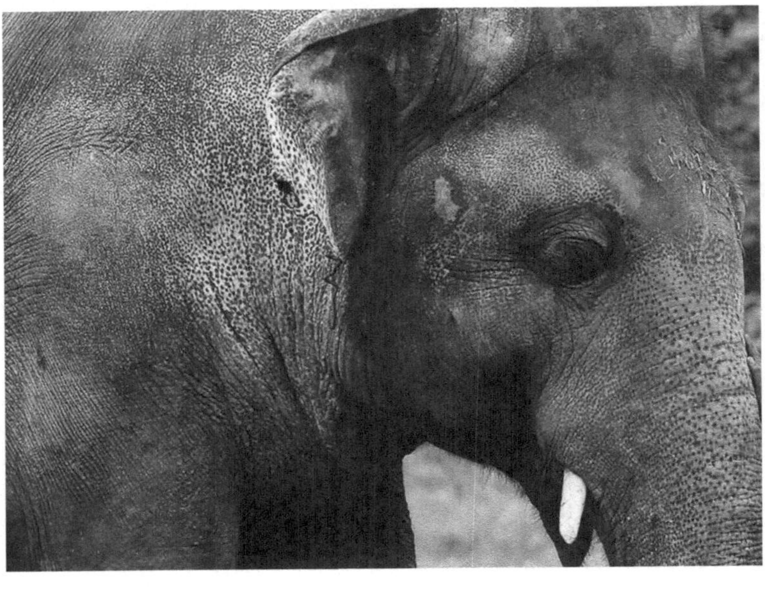

FinallyKaavan found a good refuge in Cambodia which was far from Pakistan. It was a protected forest and there were 3 female elephants who would be companions to Kaavan. So on July 17th 2020 the government of Pakistan agreed and issued an official announcement.

Preparations for shifting Kaavan after releasing was incredible. Animal lovers through out the world made elaborate preparations under the leadership of pop singer Cher. Experts visited Islamabad, checked everything and prepared a plan. 'Four Paws International' organization of wildlife expert Dr. Ameer Khaleel, and Dr. Frank Gority of "Lebniz Institute for Zoo and Wild life Research" led the team.

Encouraging through Singing

Khaleel stayed for few days with Kaavan. And took him into confidence with love and affection. He showered lonely Kaavan with immense love. Kaavan got his lost love, they became close friends. When Kaavan was depressed Khaleel cheered him by singing songs. And Kaavan liked the soothing songs and was comfortable.

"I do not have a melodious voice, I am not even a singer, still my song is loved by only Kaavan". he says, eventually it was tamed and then arrangements were made to relocate Kaavan to Cambodia. A special cargo plane landed in Islamabad, then arrived a big cage like box. Dr. Khaleel led him inside the cage by singing a song. The box was lifted by a crane and with Kaavan inside, it was placed in a truck, after a successful operation, Kaavan was shifted along with the box from the truck to the plane. Hundreds of people witnessed this with tears of joy rolling from their eyes. Everywhere the sound reverberated `goodbye Kaavan'.

November 29th 2020, Kaavan landed safely in Cambodia, He saw the two female elephants. When he was sent out of the box. He met the fellow elephants after a span of many years, he became emotional and started crying profusely. There was concrete barricade between the elephants, Kaavan pushed the trunk, between the barricade and touched their trunks and this was a touching moment. The video of Kaavan showing love to

the fellow beings went viral. Everyone who had voiced their concern in the movement rejoiced.

Khaleel stayed with Kaavan for few days. His mental and Physical wellness was taken care of. He had become obese, as there was no physical movement for so many years. He weighed 5.5 tons, so his weight was reduced, he nearlylost 50 kilos became lively and upbeat. The three female elephants, 27 year old Akrum Raas, 36 year old Kapolk and 60 year old Sreylyaam have become his companions. Now he is involved in the development of Asian elephant clan. Eventually he gained joyfilled days in his life. Animal lovers fight was a happy ending. It was a victory of humanity.

LIN WANG THE GRAND FATHER OF WORLD WAR

REMEMBERING THE WORLD'S OLDEST ELEPHANT

This is the story of a wonderful war hero 'LIN WANG' – the senior most elephant in the whole world. He was lovingly called the "Grand Father". He took active part in 2nd world war. By becoming the messenger of peace after the war, his name was synonymous with both war and peace.

When this grand father died, it was an unforgettable moment. Large number of people, nearly 1,80,000 people paid their last respects, and Taiwanese mourned for 3 days. It is common through out the world to see people mourning the death of famous personalities. But it is a rare event indeed when many people cried when an elephant died. How much they

would have loved the 'grand father' elephant! When the news of his death was announced, the president of Taiwan Chen Shui Byan expressed deep condolence and sent a wreath. The mayor of Taipe

Ma Ying-Giyu attended the funeral and declared posthumous citizenship to Lin-Waang.

"The name Lin Wang is an inspiration to us. Lin-Waang saw us growing up and we watched him growing old" said the mayor during the funeral.

The adventurous life journey of lin Waang is very impressive. He was a loving grand father of the whole country. It is a rare feat to see an elephant winning the heart of many people. He became the darling of the people of Taipae. For them he was not just an elephant, but pride of their nation. In 2003, at the ripe age of 86 years, Lin Waang died. All the leading newspapers of the country payed homage by giving wide coverage of the grandfather. Everyone cried hearing the news.

It was during the II World War and many countries were involved. Britain took active part. Japan had Captured Burma by then. The fight was going on in mountainous terrain. More elephants were employed to transport food, ammunition and other war materials to the army. At this juncture, the national expeditionary Force of China captured few soldiers from the enemy camp as prisoners of war. They also took to their custody 12 elephants that carried war materials. Our war hero Lin Vaang who was 26 year old then was one among them. The then commander of this force was general Sun-Li-Jen. After this, the elephants had to serve their new masters, so they continued to serve the Chinese army.

After the war these elephants moved with general Sun's troops. They stayed in different places for 11/2 years and then from Burma they crossed China's Kunning and Nanjing and reached Gungju city. Army soldiers trained them, they taught all the tricks learnt by soldiers, such as drills, march past, sit down and stand up exercises etc.

Further, Jen Sun moved to Taiwan in 1947. He decided to take along with him, the three loving elephants Lin Wang and 2 female elephants from their troops. After travelling for 48 hours they reached the post city Kaushiyung. From theae they were moved by train to the army head quarters. On the way one of the female elephant had died. due to fatigue, These two elephants continued to work in construction of railway lines. In 1951, another female died and Lin Wang was left all alone.

On 30th October 1954 Lin Wang was retired after a long stint in the army and he was sent to Taipae'sYounshum Zoo with honour, A 4 year old female elephant 'MAA LAAN' was brought from Japan and Lin Wang was sent there mainly to take care of this young elephant. He spent his retired life nurturing it. More people visited the Zoo, mainly to see lin Waang and they were wonderstuck when he exhibited few tricks he had learnt in the army. Especially kids pestered their parents to take them to the Zoo atleast once a week. The Zoo gained worldwide fame because more and more people came from abroad to see their loving `grandfather' elephant. People were very happy to see the way he took care of the little elephant. The Zoo was very small and the number of animals was more, it was inevitable to shift Lin-Waang to Taipaes Mujaaz. There he spent his time taking care of the young 'Maa Lan' with love and affection.

Generally elephants have a life span of 70-75 years. Lin-Wang was nearing 80s, still he was strong and well built. On October 30th he was brought to the Zoo, that day was marked as his birthday. In 1997 he celebrated his 80th birthday He was virtuous and very gentle mannered, so the people of Taipae loved him most.

The loving elephant 'Ma Laa' which lin Waang was taking care fell ill. The injury to it's leg worsened and it succumbed to death. They tried hard, but could not save her. In 2002 Ma-Laa died at the age of 54; Again Lin Wang became lonely. Through out his life he was lively and upbeat. He was not dull for once, day by day, symptoms of aging were slowly visible, he lost interest in everything, he ate less food. He started spending more time in water. On 26th February 2003 Lin Wang died at the ripe age of 86 years. He became immortal when his name was entered in the Guinnes book of world records and was honoured as the senior most elephant that ever lived. Lin Wang's skin was preserved. After persistent effort for 18 months, his replica was made using the skin and has been installed in the Zoo. It looks real and appears as if Lin Waang is standing. This could materialize because many organisations and his fans contributed, complete details, about his achievements and his long journey of life has been depicted there. The people of Taipae still remember their loving Lin Waang.

MURTHY THE KILLER

THE ELEPHANT WON BY LOVE

Once upon a time a lone tusker attacked people causing havoc in the border regions of Kerala and Tamil Nadu. People were horrified and scared to move around because this gigantic creature appeared from nowhere and continuously killed people. It had killed 28 people and this was indeed a dubious record created by a single elephant. No one knew who would be the next victim.

For many decades, in the borders of Karnataka and Tamil Nadu, near the edges of forests poacher vagabond Veerappen threatened people and instillad fear in them. No body could trace his movements So, they avoided going near the forests. He appeared

suddenly and abducted dignitaries, killed many people without reason. Even the B.S.F. soldiers could neither capture him, nor gather information about his whereabouts. Around 1990, the same situation prevailed in the borders of Kerala and Tamil Nadu. Not because of Veerappan, But because of the lone tusker which was notorious as 'Mari Veerappan' or 'Junior Veerappan"

In many villages at the edge of forests, this tusker had crushed few locals to death. It was notorious as "Serial killer". Children stopped going to school from this side and farmers could not go to their farmland and work. It was difficult for them to earn their living. People were scared even to take the sick to hospitals. It chased and killed those who came in its way. There were protests by locals. They demanded either to capture or kill the elephant. The government swung into action and tried to capture it. It could not be traced. As a last resort, the government passed orders to shoot at sight, the 9 feet tall hefty tusker.

On the one hand, the members of the family, who had lost their kith and kin welcomed this decision. But animal lovers were against this and they were shocked by the government's orders. But Kerala government was firm in it's decision to kill it. By then people had started to shoot at the tusker when they encountered. Many bullets entered it's body, still it was not afraid. The tusker entered forest and continued harassing again. Next Tamil Nadu forest department formed a team to capturing it alive and tame the killer tusker. Villagers objected to capture it alive, they wanted it to be killed, because they thought it was impossible to tame the tusker. It might even kill the mahout and forest officials if it was not killed, they warned.

But forest officials and wild life experts were ready to capture it. Dr. K. Ashokan led the team of anaesthetists and doctors. In 1998 they were successful in tracing the tusker after a long search in the dense forests near the borders of Tamil Nadu and Kerala. They administrered anaesthesia with great difficulty and captured it with the help of domestic elephants. It was then shifted to Teppakadu Madumalai elephant camp. Surprisingly they found 15 bullets stuck in its body, it was removed and medical care was provided for 2 months. Lakhs of rupees was spent for the same and it fully recovered it was put in the Kraal and trained. By feeding sugarcane and jaggery, patting it's back gently with affection, slowly they took it into confidence. It's mahout and trainer Kusumaran was effective in taking proper care of it, he controled it like a small boy and fed 'jaggery'. People named it 'Murthy' with love. For a few days, he was called "Murthy, the Killer". After many days, because of the loving efforts of mahouts, doctors and officers, from a killer, he turned out to become a gentle elephant. He learnt all the commands fast and always obeyed the mahout. After releasing from the kraal he was kept in intensive care. He was well behaved and worked with extreme loyalty. The killer elephant who had taken 28 lives became loving 'Murthy' to everyone in Madumalai camp. He started working as a Kumki elephant. Kumki or Koomkie is a term used in India for trained captive Asian elephants used in operations to trap wild elephants, or to provide medical treatment to an injured or trapped wild elephant. The term may be more specifically applied to trained female elephants used as decoys. Kumkis are used for capturing, calming and herding wild elephants or to lead wild elephants away in conflict situations. The word Kumki means "aid". An elephant has to undergo extensive training before it can become a Kumki, elephant.

Murthy, the Kumki elephant drove back the elephants that came from forests to the villages near the borders. Now he became the most loved animal in the forest department. This transformation is wonderful! Once a notorious killer elephant who had taken many lives and never even cared could be tamed just by feeding jaggery and sugarcane with love and affection. This is the power of love! Murthy, the lone tusker (Bull) is the best example to prove that; be it men or animals, those who do not bend for penalty, threats or punishments can be transformed with pure unconditional love.

HE LOVED THE ELEPHANTS SO MUCH...!

It is unbelievable! He willed his 51/2 crores worth property in the name of two elephants he loved the most. These are many instances to prove, love has no barriers of religion, country or sect. Even the puranas depict this. This is true even with animals. Among such events, the love showed by imam Aktar from Bihar is outstanding.

He had raised two elephants and loved them more than his own children. He believed. They were far, better than his family and relatives. He was happy that the elephants reciprocated his love, so he did not want them to be orphaned after his death.

It is common to see people amassing more wealth and property for their future generation to enjoy. They are not content and satisfied even when they have lots. They are more concerned in earning than doing charity. This is one of the big human weaknesses. In a rare act of love and kindness, Imam Aktar reserved his property to his loving elephants instead of his wife and children.

Along with newspapers and news channels from India, Britain's Guardian and many more papers abroad published this and the act was appreciated worldwide.

mam Aktar lived in DaanapurJanipur Village near Patna in Bihar state. He loved birds and animals since childhood. He opined that animals are much better than humans, they are loyal to their care takers and for the sake of love they even sacrifice their lives. Because of the love of animals, he had raised two elephants Moti and Rani in his house. They were very dear to him and they both loved him most and never left him even for a single day. One day a strange event happened. Many people loved Imam Aktar because he worked hard and helped people. Some people were jealous of his popularity. A few hated him because he pointed people's mistakes and was outspoken. After a long and tiring day, he went to bed. He was fast asleep, the enemies barged into the courtyard holding deadly weapons in their hands, they were about to enter his house to kill him. Seeing this, the two elephants immediately rushed to attack them. The enemies were terrified and ran away. Imam Aktar woke up due to the commotion and came out of the house. He was surprised to see the elephants chasing the enemies.

He was very much amused by this loving act. Hence forth he was more affectionate with Moti and Rani, who had saved his life. He took care of them like his own children. After this incident, he decided to give away his property worth 5 ½ crore rupees to the two elephants by will He declared Rani and Moti to be the owners of his 6.2 acres land after him. He further registered the property in the sub-registrar office in their name.

He had also mentioned that in case of the elephants death, the property would go to Airavatha Institute. He also transferred his bank balance to them. He formed a trust to look into the well being of Moti and Rani after his death. This was surprise to many.

He said "Moti and Rani are no less than my children. I have raised them with love and affection. They trust me, so it is my duty to make sure that they are not orphaned after my death, they should not starve in my absence even for a single day. For this reason I have written my property in their name. I have arranged a trust to take care of them." He found satisfaction in living with his elephants, away from his family for 10 years. He says he has found more comfort in the company of elephants rather than with his family.

He says 'it is my duty to safeguard the life of the elephants who have saved my life. They are not mere animals. They have proved that they are more dear to me than my family. So, I have appointed two servants to look after them.

HERE THE ELEPHANT SPEAKS

It is well known that elephants are emotional beings, just like us. They quietly follow orders given to them. It is common to see huge elephants following their mahouts and kavadi's with love and affection. Has anyone witnessed a talking elephant?

This is not fiction! There are many videos to testify this. One can personally witness this elephant having conversation with the mahout. Many have seen and enjoyed this rare scene. Many researchers have taken interest in this.

'Aandaal' the female elephant residing in 'Sree Ranganatha temple' in Trichi, Tamil

Nadu is the centre of attraction. Being gentle, she is the darling of Tamil Nadu. She is actively involved in the daily service of the lord in the temple, she even goes to other important temples to serve the deity. She has been in this temple for around 30 years. She wakes up at 3.30 in the morning and takes a stroll in the temple premise till 5.00 a.m. Then the temple, priest sees

that sacred Kaveri water is carried by 'Aandal' and brought in a procession to the temple and Abhishekam is performed. This is the main feature of the temple. The elephant does this work religiously without fail. Aandal was the favorite of former Chief Minister of Tamil Nadu, J. Jayalalitha. She loved Aaandal most and never missed an opportunity to meet her and spend time with her. Usually some parrots repeat and learn whatever is spoken. LikewiseAaandal can also speak.

The most interesting fact about Aandal is that she promptly responds to her Mahout Rajesh's words. Videos of Aandal speaking have gone viral several times in social media. When mahout Rajesh asks questions, she answers, though she cannot actually speak, she replies in the same tune, still everyone can understand whatever she says.

Aandaal stands beside Rajesh, when he sits in front of the temple. Rajesh caresses her trunk with love and speaks to her. This scene has been captured on camera. When Rajesh questions her "some people have come to see you, they want to take your photograph, what do you say?" She would shake her head, make certain sound and approve. This astonishing scene went viral everywhere. Forest officers, dignitaries and actors have posted this on social media. This was witnessed by many around the world and they started visiting the temple. Her speaking and responding style became well known. It is interesting to see lots of people from abroad coming to see this wonderful elephant. Rajesh and the elephant talk to each other while parading in the temple with the procession. Interestingly, after moving quiet a distance, Aandaal calls the mahout and says "Enough, let us move back" in her own tone. Elephants listening and obeying the mahout is quite common, but nowhere can we see elephant responding in the same tune. Aaandaal is the only elephant that has developed such exclusive tactfulness.

Another, astonishing factor is, she can even play the mouth organ with it's trunk. People are overwhelmed to see this rare feat. Rajesh has even taught her to play football in the temple premises. Many people visit the temple in Trichi to witness the game. After the Lord's darshan in the temple, devotees throng to see her and speak to her before they leave. A Facebook account has been opened in Aandaal's name and she has many followers, they watch and share her posts. This shows her worldwide reputation. Aandaal's little toy has been made and sold in the

temple premises. People who visit the temple do not forget to buy one and they proudly exhibit in their showcases at home.

Aandaal is well known for her tremendous patience. She never hurts anyone. She is even enjoyed, when she sees Rajesh and hugs him with her trunk. Daily she eats 150 kgs of greens and drinks 250 litres water. She rejoices when she is occasionally fed with palm leaves (Eachala Mara). And after the daily pooja she consumes the food prepared with 8 Kg rice, daal and Jaggery.

Aandaal is more than my own daughter, I cannot live without her, even for a single day, she always respects and loves me" says mahout Rajesh.

HEINOUS CRIME IN GOD'S OWN COUNTRY

PREGNANT ELEPHANT'S TRAGIC DEATH

No one expected this ghastly incident to happen in Kerala, the "God's Own Country". An innocent pregnant elephant was the victim here. People from all over the world condemned this heinous act, and this was outrageous. They could not believe how cruel humans could be. All the efforts made to save the mouthless elephant were futile with the unborn child in the womb, she died an agonizing death. The pregnant elephant was in search of food in Palakkad district, Kerala. She picked up a pineapple lying on the ground. As she started chewing the fruit, it exploded in her mouth. The elephant's mouth was blown to pieces. What a tragedy! Unable to withstand the pain, she

stood in water for 14 days without food and water. The raptured mouth began to rot, after suffering a lot finally she died. A video of this went viral on social media. Three people were arrested and an F.I.R. was filed against them. They had planted explosives in the pineapple to kill wild animals. The villagers living near the forests usually place explosives in fruits and in chunks of meat to kill wild animals for food. The ill-fated pregnant elephant became the victim of this act of cruelty. Wild life experts from the forest department managed to bring the suffering elephant out of water, but despite their efforts to save her she died. Human - elephant conflicts is common. But harming animals this way is monstrous. The conflicts have increased due to rise in the number of wild animals, human enroachment of natural elephant habitat, destruction of forests and intervention in every aspects of their life. Between 2015 and 2018, 1,713 people have become victims of human-elephant conflict in India. 373 elephants have tragically died. Even today elephants are killed by hunters and by electric lines.

THIS IS REAL WONDER!

THE ELEPHANTS WHO ATTENDED THEIR SAVIOUR'S FUNERAL

South Africa's reputed environmentalist and wild life expert Lawrence Anthony had died in his farm house. He was famously called 'elephant whisperer'. He was fascinated about animals since childhood. During war no one took care of Baghdad Zoo and the animals were orphaned there and soldiers shot and killed many animals. Being a kind hearted man he rescued the orphaned elephants and took care of them. He was saddened by their condition. Tula Tula, a small island like area, which was about 100 miles from Durban in S.Africa was reserved for protection of wildlife. He constructed a farm house and stayed there with his wife and many servants.

He took to saving wild life in the area. At that time, shooting and killing wild elephants was an exciting and a prestigious sport in South Africa. Thousand of elephants died due to this dangerous sport. Seeing this Lawrence Anthony vowed to save elephants; by protecting them in their natural habitat. He took care of the orphaned baby elephants who had lost their mothers. He saved the tuskers when they were all alone after losing their companions. Lawrence Antony effectively studied the life of elephants, when he encountered elephants he spoke with them silently and made them return without attacking him. According to him elephants do not attack humans intentionally, instead they do so when they are frightened. Lawrence Anthony was a true friend of wild elephants. He had learnt many things about elephants by experience and penned down interesting articles about elephants and received several awards. He said "when we encounter an animal, we should not directly look into their eyes, They should be taken into confidence by standing still, then we should move back with little steps, they go away without harming us."

Lawrence Anthony converted Tula tula into a protected forest and a tourist hub with the help of native tribes. Employment

opportunity was available to locals. Hunters never ventured there, because they were scared of the tribes, thus elephants were protected, and they lived comfortably. They were sure he was their protector and never harmed him. Some wild elephants loved him most, so he could go near them and even harnessed them with ease.

In March 22nd 2012 Lawrence Anthony died in his farm house. He was 61 years of age. Preparations for the funeral was underway. The body was embalmed and kept for the arrival of relatives from different places. But the following day there was a surprise. Rare guests had arrived to pay their last respects. They were none other than the wild elephants he had taken care of and protected. Many elephants came in two separate herds, walking from a jungle far away from the farm. They came, paid their last respects, wandered around the house far 2 days and mourned the death of their beloved savior. They grieved like they had lost their close relative. They shed tears, expressed sorrow and left without disturbing anyone. The people present there were stunned at this wonderful gesture of elephants. It is a mystery! How they could know about their master's death? Who had told them? How could they come from such a long distance in search of his house? It is difficult to find the answer. But these are wonders of the world. Unbelievable! But it is true. It was big news in the media. Even scientists could not find answers to this.

Elephants are ingenious animals and they are extremely sensitive, they can express their feelings like humans. They are social beings and love to be in groups. Various studies have been done on the behaviour of elephants, when an elephant in the herd dies, other elephants could easily remember the place where it died and even after many years, if they happen to pass by that place they mourn the dead. No one would have believed this if it had happened long back, they would have thought it to be fiction. But this is true and cannot be brushed aside as fiction. We might have adopted modern technology. Have knowledge of celestial objects, made advancements in science, but even now, man is unable to find answers to certain unbelievable events. The arrival of these elephants to the funeral of Lawrence Anthony is one such event which is amazing!

Elephants have sharp sense of smell. There are no other intelligent animals that can sense the smell like them. The elephants had recognized the smell of Lawrence Anthony from far, they could differentiate between the smell of a dead person. And the smell of a person who was alive. They might have learnt about his death by smell. Whatever it might be, it is amazing!

SUDEHI WHO BECAME IMMORTALISED IN HISTORY

Tahe adventures and contributions of elephants are well recorded in the pages of history. Long ago the elephants were the main strength in administration. Elephants determined the outcome of a war. It was very difficult to defeat a king who had many elephants in his army. The Ganga Rajas used these forces effectively and were famous for their strong elephants forces. Incidentally their emblem was also an elephant.

A replica of a huge elephant carrying the king with its trunk can be seen even today in front of the world famous Konark Sun Temple in Odisha. This is a testimony to one of the amazing events that occurred long ago.

Photo Credit: **Sanketh Mishra and Krishna Priye**

Narasimhadeva I was an important king of the Eastern Gangas. He had built a strong kingdom. The neighbouring states attacked them quite often. War went on for 4 years against the enemies. One day king Narasimhadeva I was badly hurt in war, and fell from the elephant. If he was caught then it would have been the end of the war. Fortunately, 'Sudehi' his beloved female elephant rushed to the spot, lifted him with her trunk and escaped from the warfield. Immediately thereafter it took him straight to the palace practitioner. Timely medical treatment was given and he was out of danger. As Sudehi saved his life, the king admired her. Sitting on the same elephant he fought many wars and won the title 'Hamira Mardhana', He was even honoured as 'gajapathi', because he had large elephant force in the army. 'gajasahani' was the chief, who led the Gangas elephants.

King Narasimhadeva I did not forget 'Sudehi' the elephant who saved his life. He carved large sculpture of Sudehi carrying him with her trunk and constructed the Konark Surya temple there. Thus he made Sudehi's memory eternal.

The Westen ganges was another strong royal family who ruled Southern Karnataka and northern parts of Tamil Nadu from 4th to the 10th century. Their emblem and the king's seal was an 'elephant'.

In the beginning their capital was Kuwalaala (Now Kolar). Then from Sripurusha's time Talakadu became the capital. Later Manne in Nelamangala taluk became a prominent 2nd capital. Sripurusha has written a book named 'Gajashastra' about the importance of elephants and about their speciality.

THE STORY OF THE STONES

THE STORY OF THE STONES

Only if we understand elephants, we can live peacefully without any conflicts. Excluding hormonal rush period, they will be normal in all situations, without considerable change in their behavior. The herd with an elephant baby or an elephant during testosterone surge will be always dangerous, accidents do happen if we ignore this. The two stone engraved elephants in the courtyard of Madikeri fort is testimony to such events.

There are two elephants sculpture in the right hand corner of Madikeri fort, they appear to be real from far, but from near it is evident that these are beautiful stone carved replica of elephants. Many tourists have taken

photographs and selfies in front of them. This stone also reminds an incident that had happened long ago. Kakemani, Kodagu's famous writer has documented this event.

It was during the reigns of Lingaraja of Haleri royal family who was ruling Kodagu. He had raised two hefty elephants, with love and affection. They were captured from Kodagu, tamed and were his royal elephants (Pattadaaane). They were placed in the shed in front of the palace. Early in the morning the 2 elephants came to the palace and trumpet to wake up the king. He gave them coconuts, bananas and caressed them. Whenever the king was free, he met the elephants and they greeted and hugged him.

It is evident from many instances that anger and irritability can bring many disasters. King, Lingaraju was short tempered. One day tragedy struck because the king was furious. The 2 elephants never came to wake him. He waited for long, there was no sign of the elephants arrival. He called his attendants and

ordered them to see what was wrong. They said the elephants were in the shed and did not wish to visit and wake him that day. The king rushed to the shed to see them. The elephants behaved strangely, they never greeted him, and tried to attack the king. He escaped and came out, he was furious and could not control his temper, in a fit of rage he ordered to shoot and kill the 2 disobedient elephants. Meanwhile the 2 elephants had even lifted a person and thrownd him far. No one dared to question the king or disobey his commands. The mahouts begged not to kill them, but the king's men did not heed to their pleas. Everyone was aware of the king's aggressive nature and short temper, and they were helpless. It was a difficult situation. The king's men did not listen. Meanwhile the shooter did his work, the two palace elephants were shot dead. The king's favorite Pattadaane were no more. The whole state mourned. There was disdain in peoples mind for the ghastly behavior of the king. Yet no one dared to express themselves and openly condemn the act. When the grumpiness subsided, the king became aware of the blunder he had committed. He had not tried to understand the behavior of the elephants before he ordered to shoot them. He repented when he learnt that the elephants behaved oddly because of harmonal rush (musth) due to testosterone surge, which was a natural phenomenon. He felt very sorry, He could not accept the fact that there were no royal elephants (Pattadaane) to greet him anymore. He was depressed because of his wrong doing and the sinful consciousness of killing his beloved elephants disturbed him a lot. He gradually lost interest in daily activities. Many elders consoled and persuaded him to engage in administration. He was not enthusiastic again, his body became weak day by day. They thought if the situation persists for long, it would badly affect the king's health. After long discussions they suggested the king to build a stone and mortar replica of the 2 elephants and place them outside the palace room, so that it could be seen from the king's room. King Lingaraja was very happy, because they looked like the two loving elephants were standing. Even now we can see them. Like this when the elephants have musth, they do not behave normally. It is up to us to understand and avoid their company.

Musth is a natural periodic condition occurring in male (bull) elephants. During a musth cycle, bulls typically experience an extraordinary harmonal surge, with their male reproductive harmone testosterone at its highest levels in the body, on average 60 times higher than their premusth levels. The condition can last anywhere from a few days, to as long as several months. This period of time is known as musth.

In spite of being peaceful animals, during elephant musth, the male becomes very aggressive. Eventhough elephants tend to be kind creatures, during this period they become temperamental. Thus even now elephants teach us a great lesson that there is a lot of difference between humans and elephants.

THIS IS THE WONDER OF DUBARE

AJJAYYA'S PROTEST IN WATER

Karnataka is famed for having largest number of wild elephants in the country, there are nearly 6,044 of them. These have earned the reputation as accomplished workers. They grow elephants in the camp will be checked when there is request for elephants. Their age, health, usefulness, which elephant can be sent to other states, which should be reaffirmed will be surveyed and decision will be taken by senior officers.

Here elephants health card will be mainly helpful. Skilled medical practitioners check elephants health on a regular basis and record in their healthcard. Experts identify and recommend the elephants to the government. They select those which can adjust to the new environment and age of the elephant is also taken into account.

Why our elephants are in such demand? Since the number of elephants has increased in our state, and human – elephant conflict is rampant, in our state permission is easily granted to capture elephants. On account of this, these are more than 100 elephants in camps. Another main reason for the demand is that, here elephants are tamed in traditional way and there are professionally trained mahouts and kavadis. Many families of the Jenu Kuruba community have grownup with elephants, they can understand elephants easily and know the art of taming them.

Domestic elephants are much disciplined in Karnataka. The mahouts and kavaadis first punish the elephants while training and they., win over them with love. Once furious elephants like

rowdy Ranga, Arjuna and others have become soft natured. Now they are actively involved in patrolling in tiger and wild elephant capture operations, transporting lumber etc. Our elephants are in demand because they are helpful in many ways. Since the age of kings, elephants have been captured and tamed. Jenu Kurubas supplied tamed animals to the Pallava kings. Though there are many elephants in other states they are not able to capture and tame them because it needs permission. There are no experts who could tame in traditional ways. Hence these is lots of demand for our elephants from different states.

Pain of Mahouts and Kavadis:

Kavadis look after the elephants like their own children. Both develop loving bond between each other. The elephants love them and the Kavadir feel sorry to leave their loving elephants. They even pray to god that their elephant shall not be sent outside.

Ajjayya who hid in water:

In 2018. 4 elephants were sent to Chattisgarh. When 3 elephants boarded the lorry, the fourth one Ajjayya refused. Ajjayya being smart, was aware of the possibility of being sent him to a distant place. So he ran and escaped when he was forced.

The mahouts and kavadi were talking about sending Ajjayya to a different state the next day. They had embraced him the previous day and wept because it was painful to leave him. Ajjayya was very intelligent, he was sure that he would be sent to a different place, so the next morning he was absconding. When they searched. he was found deep inside cauvery river with only his trunk and head visible. They pacified him by offering jaggery, banana and all the foods he was fond of, but he did not budge. He was adamant and refused to come out of water. Surprisingly he stood there crying the whole day. The Kavadis, maahuts and forest officials were sad to witness this. All the children in the colony and the employees pleaded not to send Ajjayya, they wanted to be with him But by then the formalities were completed and officials were helpless.

With great difficulty after trying hard for 2 days. Ajjayya was brought out of water. He was forcibly sent in the lorry to Chattisgarh. He cried profusely and was looking back while travelling. With a heavy heart, he left the camp. The people of Dubare remember him eventoday.

Elephants are gigantic, yet their mind is very sensitive, they are good at understanding people, and obey the commands and even respond to people. This loving Ajjayya's behavior is testimony to this. Standing in water for the whole day and the way he protested is amazing!

THE DISCIPLINED GENERALS IN DUBARE

JOYFULNESS OF Gen. CARIAPPA - THIMMAIAH

Everyone knows about General K.M. Cariappa and General Timmaiah. Both of them deserve utmost respect and adoration. Field MarshalKodanderaMadappa Cariappa OBE was the first Indian Commander – in Chief (C-in-C) of the Indian army. He led Indian forces on the western front during the Indo-Pakistan war of 1947. He was appointed C-in C in 1949. He is one of the only two Indian Army officers to hold the five – star rank of Field Marshal. His nickname was Kipper. His military career spanned almost three decades. The day Cariappa took over the reign of the independent Indian army, 15th January 1949, was marked as official army day and elaborated annually. He was born in Shanivarasanthe in Kodagu district, Karnataka.

General Kodendera Subbayya Thimayya DSO was a distinguished soldier of the Indian army who served as Chief of Army Staff from 1957 to 1961 in the crucial years leading up to the conflict with China in 1962. He was the only Indian to command an infantry brigade in battle during the second world war and is regarded as the most distinguished combat officer the Indian Army has produced. He was born in Madikeri, Coorg district. The whole world feels proud of him.

Kodagu, also known by its former name Coorg is an administrative district in Karnataka. It is known as Scotland of India, coffee cup of India and land of warriors, It is known for its serene landscape and also for the valour of its people. The district boasts of several military heroes and sports personalities. The statues of Kodava warriors can be seen in Madikeri.

In Kodagu, Cariappa and Thimayya are most respected role models. Their statues are found in many places here. They are honoured by naming buildings, colleges and roads after them.

It is interesting to see the two Generals even in Dubare Elephant camp! In Dubare, the elephant Mythili's son is named General Thimayya, Kapila's son is named general Cariappa. These two elephants are also disciplined just like the two Generals. Daily they get up early in the morning, take bath and get ready to greet the tourists. Their loving gestures mesmerizes youngsters. Without threatening anyone, they play like children. They move around with tourists and pose for selfies. The tourists feel sad when they leave the camp because they never wish to part with the Generals. Kids love them, most and they say good bye to generals and the Generals thank them by raising their trunks.

Elephants LessonsinDubare: In Dubare

The musical flow of Kaveri river, chirping of birds in the forests, elephants flirtations, cool soothing breeze; all these take us to a different world.

The main attraction of Kodagu is Dubare elephant camp. It is home for elephants which attracts tourists and is under the jurisdiction of the forest department, Dubare is an attractive tourist destination near Kushalanagara in Kodagu. There are

totally 29 elephants. General Cariappa, Gen Thimayya, Harsha, Iyappa, Gopi and other elephants live here.

The forest department takes care of these elephants with utmost care. Elephant camps are centres for domestication of wild elephants. Troublesome elephants are captured and brought to the camps. They are put in kraals and tamed. This Dubare training centre is famous in India. The forest department is worried about these trained elephants, because keeping and raising 20-30 elephants is not an easy task. All the government grants to the forest department is not sufficient to further nurture these elephants, and they could not be sent back to the forests either. At this Juncture, a new idea to attract tourists was floated at Dubare. Kaveri island is already a tourist destination, so an elephant camp was opened for these tourists. In just a few days tourists visited in large number to see elephants. Children living in cities had only seen elephants in pictures and in Zoos, but here they could even enjoy touching the elephants, caressing their bodies, feeding them banana and coconuts.

Experienced mahouts in the camp explain in detail everything about elephants. The life of elephants, the way they, are captured, how they are tamed and trained, the name of the elephants, their nature, how people harm them etc. By personally visiting the forests, visitors can watch how elephants are driven into forests and see the food they eat. Along with this, bird watching and animal safari was introduced like disciplined students, people get a chance to learn lessons about forests.

Elephant Safari has been stopped since 2 years. Still for people who stay overnight. there is a chance to witness bathing of elephants in the morning. Toursists can clean the elephants by scrubbing and feed them food with their own hands. Elephant festival was conducted once a year in Dubare. The main attractions were elephant football, elephant basketball, elephant running race etc. This was stopped when animal lovers objected.

THIS ABHIMANYU IS SPECIAL

THE FAMOUS OPERATION HERO

We are all familiar with Mahabharata's famous character Abhimanyu. He was well known for his virtue, courage, the boldness with which he rushed forward in difficult situations and his dare devil nature. In the Mathigodu camp of Nagarahole sanctuary range of Kodagu district , there is an elephant named after Abhimanyu. The name is meaningful and apt. Unlike the then Abhimanyu (Son of Arjuna) who know the art of entering the Chakravyuha (Labryinth) and did not knew the way out, our hero Abhimanyu can boast of entering, winning and coming out of the Chakravyuha. He is an able leader who is concerned about his accomplices while he returned safely.

Eventhough elephants are strong, they are fearfull of tiger, this is because tiger jump and head butt them. Whenever they encounter a tiger, they avoid confrontation and try to escape. But our hero Abhimanyu is an exception. He could stand in front of the tiger without fear. He is famously called "operation tiger expert" through out the country. Abhimanyu is called into action everytime there is threat from a tiger. He has taken part in many

successful operations to capture tigers that had killed many people and cows.

Eventhough he is smaller and has smaller tusks than Arjuna and Balarama, he is their leader when it comes to capturing wild elephants and tigers. All elephants follow him during operations.

There is demand for Abhimanyu from different parts of the country. He defeats tigers and wild elephants. Like in detective novels he finds the militants. the rude ones in his own way and captures them. He has been to many states, conducted successful operations. He has received honour and trophies, is the pride of our forest department and is respected everywhere.

In and around Bandipur area, in the year 2019, a ferocious tiger had created an atmosphere of fear and had killed 2 people. In an unusual act of bravery he captured the tiger. This ingenious and courageus act is well remembered even today by the people who had joined the operation and by the villagers. They adore him. In a dangerous situation the tiger would have killed many people if Abhimanyu was not present. It was a 5 day operation similar to Chakravyuha, and Abhimanyu was successful in capturing the tiger.

The villagers living around Bandipur area were terrified of the killer tiger who had already taken two lives. They could not

furious and it pounced, immediately Akram Pasha and Venkatesh fired tranquilizer from their guns. The tiger roared and fell to the ground. A trap was set with a net and the tiger was caught alive. "operation killer tiger" was a success..!

Wildlife expert Dr. Mujeeb says "To capture the tiger, Chakravyuha was conducted. Here the hero was Abhimanyu and his team. He was instrumental in the success of the operation and he also saved our lives".

Wild life expert Dr. B.C. Chettiappa reminisces many adventures of Abhimanyu. He had seen Abhimanyu closely in his career. According to him, no other elephant was as quick, efficient, intelligent and courageous as Abhimanyu. This is a rare trait not possessed by all elephants. He remembers Abhimanyu for 2 major events.

Tusks are important for wild elephants. Others are scared of the long and big tusks During conflicts, the elephants that possess big tusks wins. With long tusks they can easily hurt their opponents. Eventhough Abhimanyu had medium sized tusks he confronted stronger elephants.

An elephant tortured the villagers of Saavanadurga and had killed a man. When there was pressure to capture it, forest department was permitted to carry out an operation. As usual Abhimanyu took the lead. The forest was dense and hard to navigate, they waited for 2 days where they expected the elephant, but could not trace it. Finally they had to venture into the forest.

After walking for a while, Abhimanyu stopped suddenly, he warned his maahut and troops about the impending danger. The scene in front of them was terrifying. Two tuskers were ready to attack them. They were stronger than Abhimanyu and had long tusks. There was no chance for Abhimanyu to fight or

escape from them, so the officers ordered to move Abhimanyu back. But Mahout Vasanth said moving back was dangerous not only to Abhimanyu but to everyone. There was no other way to escape from the tuskers.

Abhimanyu swung into action, he took his own decision and shifted his position from slop to flat area. There was no signs of the wild elephants moving back, they were ready to attack. Abhimanyu rushed forward and head butted the two wild elephants one after the other. The elephants were shocked as they never expected this would happen. Before they could recover, Abhimanyu gave them several blows and attacked them. The wild elephants were terrified and were about to escape, by then one of them was tranquilized and captured. This incident is well remembered by medical officers Chettiappa and all those who were part of the operation.

Abhimanyu's adventures are never ending. This is another incident. A fight between two elephants in Harangi back waters had resulted in a hefty elephant getting wounded and stuck in the river for 2 days. The forest officers tried to scare him out of water but failed. Finally Abhimanyu was called, he studied the situation and entered the river with mahout Vasanth on his back. He swam towards the stuck elephant and pushed him from behind and helped him raise his legs from the sludge. By repeatedly pushing he brought the distressed elephant to the shore. This had never been done before.Like the Abhimanyu in Mahabharatha, he had all the capabalities to understand and win the Chakravyuha. He was young and being tamed, he developed all the skills of the epic hero Abhimanyu (Arjuna's Son).

He was mischievous then:

Abhimanyu was not soft natured by birth, he was very mischievous and had troubled many people. He would enter the near by villagers, eat everything to his heart's content, scared people who came near him and escaped. He was captured near Aanechoukuru in a Khedda aperation and the expert mahout from forest department Sonnappa mended him. Later Sonnappa's Son Vasanth Became his mahout. The father and son duo were Abhimanyu's friends. Vasanth grew up playing with him and happily rode on Abhimanyu's back. With mahout Vasanth on his back. Abhimanyu was eager to participate in any operation without fear, together they had captured tigers, and elephants.

Adventurous journey:

Abhimanyu participated in many operations. He captured a tusker in Sindhu Durga Maharashtra, he saved a tusker stuck in a lake near Veeranahosahalli, captured a tiger in Batheri Muthunga. Kerala, tiger operation in Metiguppe, captured wild elephant in Hassan district Aaalur Esalooru. captured a tiger in Yelandur near Chamarajnagar. captured a troublesome elephant in K.R. Nagar. Tiger operation near Maddur Zone, captured troublesome elephant in Piriyapatna and captured elephant near Polibetta.

The way he took care of his companions is highly commendable. He was more concerned about everyone else's safety in the camps and during operations. Most elephants run away with fear during operations, but Abhimanyu wonderfully encourages them and takes them along with him.There was a small baby elephant named Surya in the camp. Abhimanyu took this baby along with him to the forests and took care of him He mended, fed, put the baby to sleep and brought the baby back to the camp along with him.Ambari Aane: In 2020, he earned the title of 'Ambari elephant' 'Howdah elephant' after successfully carrying the Ambaari. (The Howdah)

THEY ARE HISTORICALLY FAMOUS

WONDERFUL DASARA ELEPHANTS

Dasara is not just a festival. It signifies victory over evil. It is a continuous historical procession, the sign of love for life and a lamp that lights the relationship between different communities. The whole state rejoices with excitement during Dasara. The unprecedented legacy wonderfully celebrated by people, celebrating is a symbol of genuine love for our tradition. It is the time when happy moments flows in everybody's heart and in every household. In particular, the excitement and enjoyment in Mysore cannot be explained. It is a treat to the eyes to see elderly and children preparing with enthusiasm for the festival. Dasara is a state

festival. It doesn't start from the palace alone, but springs from the heart of Mysoreans. They celebrate and rejoice this festival from their homes. Navaratri toys are exhibited in their house with Jamboo Savari as the main attraction. Through imagination they create miniature replica of the palace, kings, queens, the fairs and exhibit them wonderfully. This is done not to please others, but for self satisfaction, to follow our culture. and in the belief that the state would be blessed by this. Inevitably our thoughts our way of life have undergone changes over the years. In spite of global distrurbances, this belief is eternal in Mysore.

Many cultural programmes are held during Dasara. Every household participates actively. Of all the programmes the Jamboo Savari or the Elephant Procession is the biggest attractions. Dasara is not complete without witnessing this grand procession.

Mysore Dasara is the state festival also called as Nada habba celebrated in the state of Karnataka in India. Often called Navaratri, it is a 10 day festival with the last day being Vijayadashami. According to a legend, Vijayadashami denotes the victory of truth over evil. The entire city gives itself up to celebrations that include a majestic Jamboo Savari procession, dance, music and a torch light parade. The city of Mysuru has a long tradition of celebrating the Dasara festival with grandeur and pomp to mark the festival. Elephants are an integral past of Dasara. They form the core of the Mysore Dasara procession on the Vijayadashami day. The lead elephant carries the golden Howdah (Chinnada Ambari) which weighs 750 kgs and is purely made of gold. Now goddess Chamundeshwari is taken in procession on the top of a decorated elephant carrying the Howdah. Earlier the king used to sit on the elephant, in the golden Howdah and go in the procession.

The first elephant that carried the Howdah (ambari) was Jaya Marthanda, followed by Vijayabahadur, Nanjunda, Ramprasad, Motilal, Sunderraj, Gajendra, Biligiri, Rajendra, Iravata. This is evident from palace records.

Jayamarthanda: Earlier the king used to sit on the elephant. and go in the procession. After the cancellation of princely state, the practice of taking the idol of Chamundeshwari started. The first elephant to carry the Ambari was Jayamarthanda. He carried the Howdah for nearly 4-5 years, this is an incredible achievement and it has created history. He was captured from the forests of Bettadapur near Piriyapatna. Subsequently he became the most loved elephant of KrishnadevarajaWadiyar. In recognition of his service, one of the main gates near Doddakeremaidana is named after him. It is called as Jayamarthanda gate. The elephants entering the palace for Dasara are welcomed through this gate.

Iravatha: elephant has acted in the Hollywood movie 'The elephant boy' His mahout Mysore Sabu Dastagir, made his

maiden appearance in this Robert Flaherty's film based on a story by Rudyard Kipling. The film was a hit and Sabu later became a famous Hollywood hero. His subsequent films were also highly successful.

The elephant Biligiri was well known everywhere. When Jayamarthanda carried the King seated in the Howdah for the first time, elephant Biligiri was the last elephant to carry the king. He was a special elephant because, among all the elephants that carried the Howdah, he was the most gigantic, nearly 10.5 feet tall and weighed 7000 kgs. It was a treat to see him carrying the Ambari, and was like experiencing divine bliss. Everybody felt like saluting him. He had carried King Krishnadevaraja Wadiyar. The Elephant died in 1975.

Rajendra: Rajendra, oh! Kannadigas will not forget him. Famous Kannada matinee idol, Dr. Rajkumar sat on the tusk of Rajendra and sang the hit song "naavaduvanudiye Kannada nudi.." This song is well remembered by every Kannadiga, likewise the forest scene in the movie GANDHADA GUDI where Dr. Rajkumar is with the elephant Rajendra in the song is unforgettable. In this movie Rajendra mesmerized everyone. Dr. Rajkumar loved him.

Drona: Drona was one of the lead Dasara elephants of the Jamboosavari. Like the Drona of epic Mahabharatha, this elephant Drona cannot be forgotten, He carried the golden Howdah for a record 18 consecutive years between 1983 and 1997, before being electrocuted while grazing in 1998. Of all the Howdha elephants since the 20the century, he is considered the best "because he possessed an excellent ability to learn and correct himself. He was captured in a Khedda operation in the Kakanakote forest area of Heggadadevanakote in 1971. He attained celebrity status in Karnataka for it's majestic gait, grace and gentle manners. He had a perfect curve on it's back to carry the 750 kg howdah, and was the right elephant to carry the Ambari. He was 10.25 ft tall and weighed 6,400 kgs. He also acted as Tippu's elephant in the serial "The Sword of Tipu Sultan". Drona's end was tragic, whole of Karnataka mourned his death, even today many people remember him, especially during Dasara.

Balarama: True to his name, he is strong and valiant, is hefty and is peace loving. Everyone loved him. He was captured in 1987. He had carried the idol of goddess Chamundeshwari on the fabled golden Howdah for a thirteen times between 1999 and 2011 and retired.

Arjuna: He had carried the Ambari for one year after Drona. As he was responsible for the death of a mahout Arjuna was again replaced by Drona. After Drona retired, Arjuna became the ambari elephant of Mysuru's grand Vijayadashami procession, he carried the Ambari successfully till 2019 and was lauded for the same. After he was 60 years his retirement was announced by the forest department. Now after Arjuna, Abhimanyu the elephant has taken responsibility of carrying the Ambari.

OUR OLDEST GRAND MOTHERS

SHE IS THE LEADER OF ELEPHANT FORCE

A remarkable thing about elephants is that the female are the leaders. Elephants are our role models for women empowerment. There might be ferocious, troublesome and rude elephants in the herd, but the matriarch leader controls then effectively ciently. Usually the senior most female will lead the herd and all the members of the group respect and obey her. She leads the group from the front and the rest of them follow her. She would be strict at times when they disobey. Unlike humans, elephants give utmost respect to elders.

The female elephants live longer than the male, maximum being 100 years. Domestic elephants live longer than the wild ones,

because of the harsh conditions in forests, the aged wild animals cannot go in search of food, whereas aged domestic elephants are well taken care of in camps, they get timely food and medical care, so they live upto 90 years.

Female elephants are given more importance in all the camps. Especially the senior most takes care of the elephants that give birth to young ones. It is amazing to know about these elderly females. They have raised many calves with utmost care and good supervision

Karnataka has the highest number of domestic elephants, around 100 elephants in our camps. Among these the oldest will be figured out. Likewise in 2020 Ganga and Gayatri were considered elders, when the oldest dies, the next successor would be selected. The ages of domestic elephants born in camps can be known easily. But the age of wild elephants is determined by estimation. These are scientifically calculated.

Among the domestic elephants selected in 2020, Ganga and Gayatri were the oldest. On March 4th 2020 in Jaldapara National Park, Kolkata the seniormost elephant Madhubala died at the age of 90. After this 86 year old Ganga from Sakrebyle Camp in Shivamoga and 85 year old Gayatri from Bannerghatta national park camp became senior most elephants.

Gange is the leader:

In Sakrebyle Camp 86 year old Gange was the leader, Gange and Gayathri looked like twins, Those who knew them could identify them easily but strangers could not. Both were captured during Kaakankote Khedda operation in 1968. They were domesticated. Long ago trees were cut for lumber and transported by elephants. Since there were no cranes, then, forest department and locals raised elephants, for labour. Similarly Gange and Gayathri were tamed in Sakrebyle and employed to transport lumber. They were also permanent members of Dasara in Shivamoga. They walked on either side of Howdah (Ambari) carrying royal elephant. When these are besides, the Ambari elephant does not misbehave.

Gange and Gayathri were like sisters, they both were in charge of the whole camp. Gange was very strict and could mend any troublesome elephant. All the young elephants in the camp loved them most and spent more time with these grandmothers instead of their our mothers, because they took care of them with love.

"Gange is 86 year old. She is the leader of our camp. She controls all the elephants has raised many young elephants and she is very gentle" says Shivakumar, Sakrebyle Camp regional forest officer. Geetha another elephant died in December 2020 due to old age and Ganga became lonely.

Gayithri's Nature:

Gayathri who stayed in Bannerghatta was kind and gentle, she loved young elephants, had never hurt anyone and had raised many of them. She was also one of the members of Sakrebyle camp. In 2020 she was called to take part in Bannerghatta operation. The forest officials were impressed by her gentle manners, so they retained her in Bannerghatta. Incidentally she was also captured in 1968.

Gayatri became guide and mentor to 21 elephants in Bannerghatta, she held various responsibilities there. At the age of 85 years she was more brave than male elephants. She was medium built and a bit short, still the exceptional courage with which she captured the troublesome elephants was commendable. All the elephants in the camp were scared of her.

In 1968, when she was 32 year old she was captured from Balle forest.

She was then tamed with other elephants in Moorkal camp and was adopted by forest department. She then became the leader who was employed to capture the elephants who troubled a lot.

According to the forest officials, the other elephants would be disciplined and silent in her presence. All the elephants in the camp respected her.

According to Kushalappa, the deputy conservator of forests in the Camp, everyone loved Gayatri, people visited the camp mainly to see her and she welcomed them with joy. She is the grandmother not only to the elephants, but also to all the people in the Camp.

Efforts to enter her name in Guinness:

In 2016, attempts were made to add 86 year old Dakshayini's name to Guinness book of records. She was the elder elephants who belonged to God's own country's Kerala's Travancore Devasvam Board (TDB). She was the oldest living elephant they argued. But Taiwan's 86 year old, Elephant lin Waang held the record.

Nearly 1250 temples are affiliated to TDB in South Kerala, and of the 33 elephants serving in the temple, Dakshayini was the oldest. She was honoured in a public function along with her 3 retired mahouts in recognition of her seniority. A postal cover depicting her picture was released. The Travancore Royal Family had gifted her to TDB in 1949. She was considered as the world's oldest elephant, she lived a long life and died at the age of 88. Final tributes were paid to her in Mahadeva Temple Chegallur, Kerala.

Remembering Indira:

82 year old Indira who was in Sakrebyle Camp is unforgettable. She was the oldest elephant in the camp. Her exact age was not known, so attempts were not made to include her name in Guinness records. She fell ill and died in 2017. She was member

of the camp for nearly 50 years. Many people and wild life experts says, she had crossed 85 when she died in 2017. It was a record, many people cried. Her Mahout Jaleel Ahmed says "I feel like, I have lost my family member, she has seen 5 mahouts, no one has seen her getting angry. Visitors could meet her without fear or hesitation. In 1968 she was captured from Kaakanakote forest. Gange and Geetha had influenced her nature."

There are similarities between human and elephants nature. It is amazing to Observe their family relations and the behaviours of elephants. Aunts and grand parents role is pivotal in nurturing the young ones among elephants. We humans always love grandparents more than our parents because they always tell bed time stories, hug us, prepare delicious food, crunchy snacks and never ever scold when we are troublesome. We always love to be with them. Likewise even among elephants. Grandparents are youngone's favorite. The mother elephant will be relieved of her responsibilities when grand parents are around.

Elephant herd is like a family and elder female is their leader. She manages all kinds of responsibilities like assisting in baby deliveries, raising youngones and teaching them life skills.

When the female elephant becomes pregnant, the grandmother takes care of her. All the members of the family monitar her, become vigilant and take care of her wellbeing. The way they behave during childbirth is amazing.

During deliveries all the male elephants move away and make sure not to allow anyone near the mother, a sort of guarding the place. The rest is taken care of by the grand mother. She will be near the pregnant and instill courage in her. She keeps the infant from getting hurt when it comes out. The other female elephants surround the mother and form a shield till the baby stands on its feet, and they make sure that calving of elephant is not visible outside.

LOVE IS THE ANIMALS ONLY LANGUAGE

The hero Somu is the caretaker of animals in Mysore Zoo. He takes care of orphaned baby elephants. He has exceptional talent of understanding animals, their language, feelings and he can even study their mind effectively. He offer motherly love and affection to the baby elephants he nurtures.

"Love is the only animal language" Animals can be won easily with love". This is what Somu always said about elephants. I liked Somu's words very much. With these words a whole books can be written. We can analyse this sentence in different ways with our own perspective. What I liked most is the loving reaction to his own experience with animals.

Somu is not well read, he is an innocent boy who lives with animals. He doesn't have any human companionship, he always lives with elephants and is expert in taming them. Unlike with humans, animals world is full of love that is genuine. There is no fake or selfish love here. With pure love we can communicate with animals, Can understand their feelings. They can be won with true love and they can even become friends with us.

Somu is an animal lover who takes care of especially orphaned elephants. He has been gifted with an exceptional talent. He can understand animals, their feelings, their language and study their mind effectively. He is very affectionate and gives motherly love to the small orphaned baby elephants. The main attraction in Mysore Sri Chamaraja Zoo is baby elephants. Not only elephants live with their mothers, there is an orphanage for animals in Zoos where orphaned animals are nurtured, protected and educated. Here Somu is the caretaker and protector of the orphaned baby elephants. With utmost love and affection he takes care of orphaned baby elephants that are brought from forests, villages bordering forests and also from camps. Likewise there are 4 orphaned baby elephants in Mysore Zoo. Immediately after they were born, few were separated from their mothers. They are Ishvarya, Kollegala, Madesha and Chamundi. These are orphans deprived of mother's love. So Somu is their mother now. Somu is good at attracting them with kind words and love. It is amazing! Within 2 days baby elephants become close to Somu like with their own mothers. They start their day by seeing Somu. He should feed them milk with feeding bottle, remove lices or worms from their bodies. Even in the afternoons Somu should feed them with his own hands. They feel comfortable in holding Somu's legs with their little trunks.

They go near him and cuddle him which is a heart touching, scene. They hold his hands with their tiny trunks and go for walk thrice a day. It is treat to the eyes to see these tiny tots playing with Somu in Mysore Zoo.

Somu loves them very much he says "I haven't felt they are elephants. I am raising them like my own children or my sisters and brothers. To tame an animal is much easier than discipling humans. Because people can change their behaviours any time. But once they start to love, animals do not betray". Somu's words are meaningful.

"Show them unconditional love, immediately they start to love you. Because love is their only language it is false notion to think it is impossible to understand animals. If we continuously love them, their feelings are understood. Baby elephants are more intelligent than us".. he says.

What Somu says is true. The satisfaction and contentment we get in the company of animals, in their care, in loving them, we cannot get even amidst 100 people. Somu is a real example to testify this. These babies talk to Somu in sign language. They know their wants and needs. Though there are many elephants in the Zoo, these orphaned baby elephants love to be in Somu's arms. For them Somu is a dearest friend, be all end all.

NO DISCRIMINATION FOR FRIENDSHIP BETWEEN ELEPHANTS AND HUMANS

During the period of Jayachamaraja Wadiyar, the king of Mysore loved his royal elephant. The mahaout was Sabu alias Abdul Khader. The mahout and the elephant were like close friends, very affectionate to one another. One day this elephant had hormonal surge. In a fit of rage unknowingly it hurt his loving mahout Abdul Khader badly.

This is a natural periodic condition known as musth occurring in male (bull) elephants during this cycle, bulls typically experience an extraordinary hormonal surge, with their male reproductive hormonetestosterone levels increasing to higher levels. They become temperamental and very often aggressive.

Instances are many when musth elephants have killed their mahouts. It is a biological condition and lasts for upto three months. Here the mahout had never seen the elephant's behavior during musth, so he never expected this to happen. Sabu was severely injured, was carried to the hospital and admitted, he returned home after few days of medical care.

After the hormonal surge subsided, the elephant came to normal. It became tensed without seeing his dear friend Sabu, the mahout. Daily he waited for him near the door of the elephant shed. When the mahout never turned up the elephant was depressed and stopped eating food. The caretakers of the elephant were worried. Doctors came and investigated, nothing was wrong they said. Everything would be alright after a few days they thought. But the elephant which starved became weak. They worried they might lose the elephant if the situation prevailed. So they brought to the notice of the Maharaja, Jayachamaraja Wadiyar. When he came to know about the sad condition of his beloved elephant, the maharaja was worried. He personally visited the elephant shed. He told to remove the chains that was tied to the elephant. No sooner did the chain was untied, than the elephant rushed outside and walked straight toward the main road. Onlookers were scared, some left the place thinking the elephant again had hormone surge, but it never harmed anyone. From the main road it came to Agrahara, from there headed towards Nanjumalige and went straight to the Mahout's house. It stood outside and inserted the trunk through the door and searched the house. Mahout was sleeping inside, he heard the noise around, came out and saw his friend elephant calling him. He forgot all the pain, and his illness did not matter to him. He came out of the house, hugged it's trunk and started to cry. The elephant also cried; the people around joined both of them. What an emotional scene! Wonderful act of love! Great friendship! And a beautiful relationship! It was.

The mahout had brought his elephant home previously several times. He would tie the elephant in front of his house when he came home to rest. Thus the elephant was familiar with the way to mahout Sabu's house. Now the mahout sat on the elephant and came to the palace. There the elephant thanked the Maharaja with gratitude, may be because he got his friend back. This is indeed unforgettable!

This is an interesting incidence remembered by K.M. Chinnappa, a retired forest officer in his book 'Kaadinolagondu Jeeva'. 'A life inside a forest'.

He never mentioned the name of the elephant. The mahout was a habitual drunkard. He took his elephant when he went out and made it drink along with him. After drinking heavily, the mahout was unable to walk and used to fall down. This elephant carried daily, brought him to the camp and put him to bed. What a strange relationship! Similarly, an elephant named Jinnah went silently to eat harvest crops. Till he reached the fields, he held the bell tied to the neck with his trunck so that the bell could not make sound. An intelligent elephant indeed!

THE ELEPHANTS LOVE OF KANNADA

Kannada is the language of Karnataka state Complaints are abounding that most Kannadigas do not speak in Kannada, here. Other languages are used more than Kannada. Here is an interesting story of elephants, that moved away from Karnataka and have made Kannada their mother tongue.

Karnataka is ranked number one with the highest number of elephants in the country. Because of human – elephant conflict, many elephants have been captured here. More than 100 domestic elephants are there in various camps in the state. So there is more demand for these elephants from other states. Likewise in 2008, 8 elephants from

Bandipur, 8 from Dubare camp, 3 from Mathigodu camp were sent to Uttar Pradesh and Chattisgarh. The elephants thus sent are able to adopt to the new environment with in a few days. They will travel long distances by trucks with their mahouts and will be tired, again after resting for few days they come back to normal. The mahouts return leaving the elephants with the new mahouts there.

After setting in the new environment, they adjust to the new place, but they faced a different problem with the new language there. Here our mahouts spoke with elephants only in our language, Kannada. They gave command in Kannada The mahouts communicated in their own way and the elephants obeyed them. When sent to other States, they adjusted to the new mahouts, but were not comfortable with the language that the new mahouts spoke. Attempts were made to adjust the new command language. But the elephants refused to learn the new language. Finally our mahouts stayed with them for 3 months in the new state, taught the mahouts Kannada and returned. Sometimes few mahouts even visited our state, stayed for few months, learned Kannada for elephant's sake, learned the command language by writing Kannada in Hindi or in their mothertongue. After learning they returned and gave command to our elephants only in 'Kannada'. Now mahouts speaking Kannada is common in the camps of other states.

This is very interesting and elephants are our role models when it is love for our mother tongue. 'Kannada'. Our elephants who have settled outside Karnataka have made Kannada their loving language.

Nanjunda, the Kaavadi from Mathigodu camp says "I had been to Chattisgarh with the elephant Gange. The mahouts there tried to take control of the elephant in their language, she did not budge.

She did not respond to the new language. Finally the mahouts could win over the new elephants by learning the language. The elephants loved most. I saw the elephants sent there from Karnataka, stuck to Kannada, their own language".

Dr D.N. Nagaraj, wild life expert says "now domestic elephants sent from our state did not obey the command other than Kannada. So inevitably the mahouts had to learn Kannada for their sake" our mahouts stayed there for 3 months, taught them Kannada and returned".

LOVE FOR KANNADA Gange:

In Mathigodu elephant camp, almost all the elephants love Kannada. They learn the language by hearing the Kaavadis, the mahouts and their family speaking Kannada. So, many mahouts teach the command soon in Kannada. Because of this they love their language. Especially elephant Gange, sent to Chattisgarh from Mathigodu is more particular about Kannada language. She loves her language the most. She never responds to any other language commands other than Kannada. Only if called in pure Kannada, she comes, if asked to stand or any action is called for, it should be ordered only in Kannada She was wellknown in the camp for her love for Kannada language. She was not happy when she was sent to Chattirgarh. No one wished to part with her either. Gange's 2 year baby stayed in Mathigodu in her memory who is been trained in Kannada. She responds happily when called in Kannada say the staff of the camp with love.

CAMP ELEPHANTS IN NEED OF COMPANIONS

THE PAIN OF SEPARATION

Male elephants always long for companionship with female elephants. They roamed freely with them in forests. After these wild elephants were tamed and domesticated these elephants do not have companions, so they are mentally and physically disturbed. Domestic elephants have sumptuous meals, have many caretakers, they receive royal honour during dasara festival.

In a way, the male long for female company and if they don't find companions in the camps, they escape into forests in search of females. Retaining them in the camps is difficult for the staff. Moreover these elephants are under risk in the forests. In the 7 camps in Karnataka

there are 79 males and 24 female elephants. This is one of the reasons for them to escape into forests.

There are more than 100 domestic elephants in our camps. The most important Camps in our state are Dubare and Mattigodu in Kodagu, Sakrebyle in Shivamogga, Rampura in Chamarajanagar district. There are in total 30 elephants in Dubare camp. 28 male and 2 female ones. When the males have hormone surge (musth), there are no females to control them and so they become dangerous.

Elephants go to forests in search of female companions when they have (musth) testosterone rush and it is difficult to stop them from leaving. In few instances, when they are tied, they have attacked the mahouts and fought fiersely with other elephants. So they could not be tied and retained in the camps. When they are allowed to graze, they escape into the forests and roam in search of companions, pick a suitable female, broods for a few

days with the female and after the hormone surge subsides, it returns to the camp. When these domestic elephants are in the forest, wild elephants try to attack them. The tuskers recognize these elephants, round it off, form group and attack them. In this way many elephants were seriously injured. So these cannot be left in the jungle for long.

Likewise it is dangerous if there are female elephants in camps, because wild tuskers rush to the camps in search of them and attack the domestic elephants. In Nov 15, 2018, 57 year old elephant Rajesh was dead in Dandeli camp, the same had happened even in Nagarahole forest. Because of this female elephants are not kept in camps. Even if they are captured, they are left away in forests.

Eventhough there are females in camps, they do not easily accommodate these males. When they have testosterone surge (musth), the males doesn't like the females in the camp, so they escape to the forests in search of strong females there. So the elephants in the camps depend on elephants in the forest for their companionship.

The ratio of males to females in the camps

Camp	Male	Female	Totle
1. DUBARE	28	2	30
2. DODAHARAVE	1	4	05
3. BALLE	22	3	25
4. SAKREBYLE	16	8	24
5. DANDELI	1	1	02
6. RAMPURA	10	6	16
7. K. GUDI	1	0	01
TOTAL	**79**	**24**	**103**

THE PLANTATION ELEPHANT CLAN

THE WILD ELEPHANTS WHO HAVE NEVER SEEN THE WILD

Elephants mainly live in forests. Sometimes even if they come to villages in search of food, they have to return to forests for reproduction, food patterns, wandering, their way of life and everything else happens in forests. Though some wild elephants are captured from forests, tamed and domesticated, they are kept in camps that are at the edges of forests. These tamed elephants from the camps are allowed daily to roam in the forest. Even though they are out of forests they find it difficult to adjust to village life.

But surprisingly there are different type of elephants which have not seen forests at all, they are not the ones found in Zoos or

circuses. They reside near the borders, still they do not go inside forests. These are elephants that are born, brought up and reside in coffee plantations. Each year their number is increasing. I call them plantation elephants. Among wild and domestic elephants, off late this new offspring the plantation elephants are creating problems for coffee planters and the forest department.

When wild elephants that live in forests are tamed, they become domestic elephants. Their offspring also continue to be domestic and can be easily tamed. Before, few elephants visited the villages often for many reasons, stayed for few days and returned to the forests. But now the situation is different. These elephants, instead of going back, roam from one plantation to the other, they make coffee plantation their home and are giving birth to cubs here. Amazingly these babies never see the wild in their life time, they grow in plantations, sometimes if they are driven to forests they refuse to go. They are scared of forests, so they return to plantations. Because of these cubs, the elder ones also stop visiting forests and they stay back in plantations and become permanent plantation elephants. We can find many such elephants in Kodagu. Even in Hassan. Chickkamagalur,

Shivamoga and many more districts, plantation elephants are found in large numbers. Earlier wild elephants came to farms and fields in the night and returned to forests in the morning. Because they are born in coffee plantation, they have adjusted to plantation life, these elephants could not be driven to forests; even if they are forced, they return to their original place which is the coffee plantation says Manoj Kumar I.F.S. Officer who was the Chief Conservator of forests of Kodagu district.

The plantation elephants eat jackfruit, areca, coconut, bamboo, banana, sugarcane and all that are available there. They depend on lakes and bays for water. When they do not find jackfruit and other crops, they started to eat coffee harvest. This was confirmed from the coffee beans found in the elephant faces.

These plantation elephants are not as dangerous as wild elephants that occasionally visit villages. Because they live in plantation, because of their proximity to humans and they are familiar with human smell they have easily adjusted to the new environment away from forests. When they give birth to young ones, when they have hormone surge or when people scare them unnecessarily, they fearfully attack to protect themselves, especially when crackers are burst in plantations to drive elephants, they are terrified says Dr. Umashankar, wild life expert.

Generally these plantation elephants do not harm coffee plants. But they are lost and run hither and thither, when crackers are burst, they creat havoc in the plantation and they destroy coffee plants says Chengappa from Palangala.

When wild elephants are driven, they return to forests, once scared they do not venture into villagers. But plantation elephants that are born and brought up in plantations find it difficult to adjust to forest life. Because of this their mind gets agitated so they try to attack when they are terrified.

It is estimated that nearly 200 to 300 wild elephants are likely to be present in coffee plantation of Kodagu. Among them nearly 30 to 50 cubs were born in plantations. These elephants do not trouble the forest department, because they are permanent members here. Because of these elephants plantation workers are scared to come and work in coffee plantations, so work is delayed at the plantations. Because of this delayed work, there is considerable drop in yield of harvest crops and consequently decline in income, this is the main difficulty faced by coffee planters. Studies are done by the forest department to find solution to this new challenge.

CHANGES IN FOOD HABIT

THE WILD ELEPHANTS NEW FAVORITE FOOD

The food patterns of wild elephants are undergoing tremendous change. We humans slowly adjust to the food patterns of the place in which we live for a long time. Likewise, of late the food patterns of wild elephants that are constantly entering the villages is undergoing considerable change. They have started eating the bitter coffee harvest. Before they barged into coffee plantations and destroyed coconuts and bananas, but now they are eating coffee in large quantities. This has adversely affected the coffee industry and the growers are worried. Natural disasters, falling coffee prices and many other problems were faced by the

coffee industry, now wild elephants are creating new problems. The wild elephants wandered into the coffee plantations and threatened the owners and workers. The coffee industry shudders because elephants are directly destroying the harvest crops. The people around Chikkamagalur, Hassan and Shivamoga districts are helpless because there seems to be no solution to this problem. It has caused anxiety among them.

In 2007, studies were conducted by experts for 4 years in and around Kodagu, in the areas where coffee is grown. They were surprised to see small quantities of coffee seeds in the faeces of elephants. Nowadays, coffee itself is the main staple food for many wild and plantation elephants. Minimum 2 kgs of coffee beans were found in their faeces. In the beginning, the elephants were occasionally eating coffee beans, but then after gradually adopting to coffee plantation life, they have changed their diet. This is a big challenge to the coffee industry. It is one more addition to human – elephants conflict.

Because of these elephants, coffee plants and banana plants grown near the houses have almost vanished to a large extent. No one is ready to plant new ones because they fear the elephants.

As a result of this areas with banana plants are disappearing. So the elephants face shortage of food in the villages. Inevitably they started eating ripe coffee beans say the experts.

Nanda Subbaiah, the president of Kodagu's Siddapura coffee growers and small farmers association says "The elephants are not only eating from the plantation, they also come in the night and eat the coffee piled up in the yard, which is collected and brought from the garden plantations. They find it easy to eat piled up ripe coffee beans which are available in large heaps. So instead of piling up, we are spreading coffee beans in the yard so that it becomes difficult for them to pick up the spread beans from their tusks".

According to new findings and from researches conducted by few growers and experts from the coffee growers association. 20% of coffee is lost because of these elephants.

There is demand for coffee beans produced from elephant faeces all around the world including Brazil. The locals do not like to drink such coffee, so it has to be exported; and is more profitable. Like the wild eat or boar faeces coffee beans, this too has to be encashed profitably.

GOLD'S PRICE FOR ELEPHANT COFFEE

Long ago it was big news when elephants wandered in towns. They ate bananas, coconuts, sugarcane and returned to forests. Newspapers reported about the destruction they caused in detail. People used to visit the place as if it were a tourist spot. The villagers were anxious and it was cause of concern and also wonder to see the elephants wandering around. But now the situation has changed completely. It is common to see elephants coming to town and they have become part of society. People talk about the arrival of elephants and discuss casually about its movements. No attempt to drive them was successful. When they were sent back to

forests, they would reappear in the same areas after a few days. When the forest officials read the reports from news papers, about the harassment by elephants, they used to rush to the spot immediately and take action. But now, even if they are called, they only ask about the number of elephants. Because in most of the villagers at the edge of forests, movement of elephants is common.

I have seen people searching the footprints to confirm the arrival of elephants. Experts studied the foot prints and estimated the number of elephants that had arrived, the size of the elephants, the number of young ones accompanying them, the direction where it moved, the time they returned back and many more.

But times have changed, the search for the foot print was long gone. Now it is time to look for it's faeces! which is much valuable it is gaining more significance in our country. In coffee plantations abroad growers never worry if the fruits fell from coffee plants, they are very much behind the elephant faeces. They do not allow anyone to touch the drop, because it is gold price for seeds mixed with the faeces. Drink the coffee made from these seeds..! Ah! What however! Wonderful taste..!

Why? It is nauseating? It is true, we can scoff at this coffee now, but in the near future, we are not far away from high demand. Abroad, this coffee is in much demand now it is expensive and famous..!

Coffee prepared from these beans is full of flavor and tastes good. It is learnt that when the wild elephants eat coffee, it will stay in their stomach for 10 hours mixing with the other food inside. During this period, protein rich ingredient and other properties add, especially if the seeds they consume is ripe and is of good quality, good seeds are accumulated.

Until recently, the wild elephants barged into plantation, broke and ate coconut, banana, areca and palm trees, when they moved around they would destroy the coffee plants and return back to forests. But, for a few years now, the elephants have been staying in the plantations without returning to the forests. When they could not find areca, coconut and palm they started eating coffee. Because of this coffee growers are facing severe anxiety. Coffee harvests are also lost along with the plantations.

The seeds obtained from the faeces of coffee eating elephants is in much demand in abroad. In Kodagu, Chikkamagalur, Hassan and many more Coffee growing areas, some people buy these crop beans and send overseas, it seems to become a profit making business in the near future. Ramesh, a coffee planter from Kodagu has a plantation in Siddapura. There are many elephants who have made their home here. He has collected their faeces. His son stays in America where there is much demand for this coffee beans from his friends there. So he requested his father to send the beans. Thus for the first time there was a huge demand.

Even the faeces of coffee eating elephants found in forests is collected by tribals living there, and they give away this valuable product to people.

The coffee seeds found in the faeces of coffee eating wild cats is already in demand. Now the wild cats are less in number and much seeds are not available. Elephant faeces seeds are in higher demand and cost more than the wild cat seeds.

This type of elephant seeds had been collected abroad. Moreover they feed domestic elephants with food mixed with ripe coffee beans. They collect the beans from their faeces and make profit by selling the beans.

The coffee growers are not worried about elephants eating their coffee beans; they are worried that the elephants might defecate these beans outside their plantations.

THE OLD DOMESTIC ELEPHANTS OF KERALA

THEY LEFT THE ELEPHANTS IN THE KODAGU FORESTS

Kodagu is located in the borders of Kerala. Oflate it is facing a different kind of problem. The temples of God's own country Kerala have many domestic elephants. When there became old they drive them into the forests. And from the forest these old elephants enterd the villagers that lie in the borders of Kodagu.

Many private persons also raise elephants, few owners think it useless to keep old domestic elephants, so they drove them to the forests; these old elephants enterd coffee plantations and forests of Kodagu in search of food and stay there. Because of this, along with wild elephants and plantation elephants, this new group which is neither wild nor domestic has been created. The forest department is confused because there is no specific official information regarding this now group of elephants. But the farmers and the coffee planters who were fed up could testify this argument. They could find more than 20 such elephants. To supplement this, a wild elephant with a rope tied to its neck and a female elephant that came from forest with a bell tied to her neck were traced.

Before there were no strict rules in Kerala to raise elephants. Almost all temples had elephants. There are many timber merchants who keep elephants to assist them and also rent it out for different functions. But now the government has issued regulations over raising elephants and to obtain licences. It is mandatory to provide details of elephants they own and an identification chip is installed.

Licence is obtained once the details of the elephants is provided. So few of them hid their old elephants that did not have licence from the forest department. After issuing licence, the department sees that the owners nourish the elephants till the end. In case the elephants die, it should be brought to the notice of the department. They would be relieved only after an inspection. Instead of taking licences, poeople are driving the old elephants into the forests secretly. People who have licences, also drive them into forests and say their elephants were missing. In the past, they made profit when the elephants could transport timber. Demand for elephants fell when cranes arrived. Because of excessive pressure from environmentalists and wild life lovers, they thought it was better to leave in the forests rather than rearing them. Usually females are left in the forests, as they are more people friendly, they cross borders and enter coffee plantations. They go around houses without harming the villagers, they eat to their hearts content, wander freely for a while and return along the same way. They like the smell of human beings so avoid going to the dense forests.

Kedamallur is a village in Kodagu's Virajpet taluk. It is located in the borders of Kerala. A wild elephant with a bell tied around the neck was found destroying harvest crops. It also had a tied mark on its leg. People in the surrounding coffee plantations escaped when they heard the elephant approaching them. Surrounding Yuvakapadi village, locals complained the department that they saw elephants with similar tied marks.

According to Manoj Kumar, Who was Kodagu circle chief conservator of forests, people complained about elephants entering our forests from Kerala and they had a doubt that they are still roaming in Kodagu villages. So these should be captured.

The owners should take care of their elephants. Only with prior permission elephants can be left in the forests. Since these elephants were in contact with humans, they might have contacted many diseases. Including Tuberculosis. If left in the forests directly there is a risk of the disease spreading to wild elephants. So environmentalists insist thorough health checkup should be done to these elephants. Now with the help of villagers, the staff of forest department are busy searching for these domestic elephants, in Kodagu plantations and also around the forests.

finding the owner through Chips:

A new order has been issued to install a chip to all domestic elephants. The chips include the details about the owner and the elephants in the forest department camps, with private and temple bred elephants. The full details will be visible when the chip is scanned. It is impossible to find the owners if there is no chip say officers in the forest department.

THE LEADER'S TRAGIC STORY

SHE DIED PROTECTING HER HERD

This is the tragedy of an elephant who died while rescuing her herd. As their leader, when the members of her group collapsed in front of her, she rushed to protect them, but she became the victim.

4 elephants had died due to electric shock in the coffee plantation, the leader of the group was one among them. 40 elephants had lived in Siddapura Tata estate and the surrounding farms. They never wished to go back to the forests, so they found their home in this section of the coffee plantations and they became plantation elephants. Among them, there was an elder female elephant who led the group. She was a capable leader

who had complete knowledge of all the plantations in the area and all the possible routes. This was well known to the forest staff. This leader had appeared in various places, so in order to keep track of her movements the forests officials had planned to install radio collar to her. This female was not dangerous, and she never harmed people, instead she led the herd away from the township area. Similarly she was the leader to a group of nearly 13 elephants. Usually elephants follow their leader, they obey and behave as per her orders. She controls the rude ones, and keeps the youngers ones always in the herd, so that they are not missed out. She always decides the route in which they should move.

Out of experience, she was able to guess when and where the food crop was available which was safe, which was unsafe being intelligent and the senior most, she would rush to protect her herd when they were in dangerous situations.

That particular day, this herd had been to Kodagu's AmmattiKannamangala section. Most rainy days in Kodagu are dangerous. The downpour will be continuous get frightening. Due to hurricanes, trees as well as houses get washed away. When the wind blows, trees fall on live electric wires and it would be dangerous. Many people in Malnad have lost their lives due to electrocution by stray wire. Due to heavy rain and fierce wind, electric wires broke and fell on the ground. It was a low tension wise used to supply electricity to houses; even when they fall down electricity passes through the wire. Two of the elephants in the group stepped on a live wire and they were electrocuted. The leader who was away from these elephants, sensed danger and immediately rushed to save them. She pulled the live wire, but she was electrocuted.

Victims fall into their sleeping position when there is electrical accident. Among the dead elephants, the three were in this position, the dead leader elephant was in squatting position, which meant it had come to rescue the group members.

Elephants also respond emotionally. They mourn the victims of the accident. Not only that, in this way, while wandering if they happen to cross the accident spot they stand where their companion had died and grieve. Many people have witnessed this. This has been seen by the tribal people who live in the forests.

The remaining 9 elephants of the same group walked there till the following morning. Eventually, they returned with a heavy heart, realizing that their companions were no more. Few people saw these 9 elephants grieving.

Usually the tusker maintains fair distance from the group. They love to be alone. The group is always controlled by the female, thus elephant's life is female oriented. The harmless leader who tried to protect the members of her group was one of the victims of this electrical accident. It is a tragedy that in a span of 15 days, 6 elephants were electrocuted.

ಐತಿಚಂಡ ರಮೇಶ್ ಉತ್ತಪ್ಪ ಅವರ ಕೃತಿಗಳು

1. ಪತ್ತ್‌ಕಥೆರ ಪುತ್ತ್ (ಕೊಡವ ಸಣ್ಣಕಥೆ)
2. ಜೂಂಗ್‌ನ ಬದ್‌ಕ್ (ಕೊಡವ ಕಾದಂಬರಿ)
3. ಉಮ್ಮತ ಪೂವ್ (ಕೊಡವ ಕಥಾ ಸಂಕಲನ)
4. ಪೂಮಾಲೆ ಕುಡಿಯ (ಸಂಶೋಧನ ಗ್ರಂಥ)
5. ಭಕ್ತರತ್ನಾಕರ ಕೀರ್ತನೆ (ಅಪ್ಪಚ್ಚಕವಿಯ ಹಸ್ತಪ್ರತಿ ಸಂಪಾದನೆ)
6. ಚದ್‌ಚಿಯಾ ಚಂಜಾದಿ (ಗ್ರೀಕ್ ನಾಟಕದ ಅನುವಾದ)
7. ಬೆಟ್ಟದ ಹಾವು (ಬಿಳಿಗಿರಿರಂಗನಬೆಟ್ಟದ ವಿಸ್ಮಯ)
8. ಗಿಡದ ಮಾಯೆ (ವಾಸ್ತುಗಿಡದ ವಿಸ್ಮಯ)
9. ಕೊಡವ, ಒಂದು ಸಾಂಸ್ಕೃತಿಕ ಅಧ್ಯಯನ (ಸಂಶೋಧನ ಗ್ರಂಥ)
10. ಒತ್ತತಕ್ಕ್ (ಲಲಿತ ಪ್ರಬಂಧ)
11. ನಲ್ಲತಕ್ಕ್ (ಲಲಿತ ಪ್ರಬಂಧ)
12. ಕುಡಿಕಾರ (ನಾಟಕ)
13. ಗದ್ದಿಗೆ ವಿಸ್ಮಯ (ಆಧ್ಯಾತ್ಮಿಕ ಕೃತಿ)
14. ಕೊಡಗಿನ ಕಾಳಿದಾಸ (ಅಪ್ಪಚ್ಚಕವಿ ಅಧ್ಯಯನ ಗ್ರಂಥ)
15. ಕೊಡಗಿನ ಮಹಾವೀರ (ಸ್ವಾ.ಲೀ. ದೇವಯ್ಯ ಅಧ್ಯಯನ ಕೃತಿ)
16. ಕೊಡವಾಮೆಕ್ ಬಂದಲಕೆ (ಕೊಡವ ಚಿಂತನಾ ಗ್ರಂಥ)
17. ಬಲ್ಲಾದೆ ಪುದುಮೆ (ಕೊಡವ ಲಲಿತ ಪ್ರಬಂಧ)
18. ಕೊಡವರು ಹಾಗೂ ಕಾವೇರಿ (ಅಧ್ಯಯನ ಕೃತಿ)
19. ಕೊಡಗಿನ ಗಾಂಧಿ (ಅಧ್ಯಯನ ಕೃತಿ)
20. ಕುಂಞಿ ಪುಟ್ಟ್‌ನಲ್ಲಿ... (ಸಾಂಸ್ಕೃತಿಕ ಅಧ್ಯಯನ ಕೃತಿ)
21. ದಿವಾನ್ ಚೆಪ್ಪುಡಿರ ಪೊನ್ನಪ್ಪ (ಅಧ್ಯಯನ ಕೃತಿ)
22. ಪಡೆಬೀರ ಕುಲ್ಲೇಟಿರ ಪೊನ್ನಣ್ಣ (ಅಧ್ಯಯನ ಕೃತಿ)
23. ಕೊಡಗಿನ ತಲ್ಲಣ (ದುರಂತದ ಹಿಂದಿನ ಸತ್ಯಗಳು)
24. ಮೀದಿ ಬೆಪ್ಪೊ (ಕೊಡವ ಸಾಂಸ್ಕೃತಿಕ ಅಧ್ಯಯನ)
25. ಮತಭಿಕ್ಷೆ, ಅದಿ ಅನ್‌ಟೋಲ್ಡ್ ಸ್ಟೋರಿ (ರಾಜಕೀಯ ಸಾಹಿತ್ಯ)
26. ದಿ ಟಾಕಿಂಗ್ ಎಲಿಫೆಂಟ್ (ಆನೆ ಲೋಕದ ವಿಸ್ಮಯ)